Please enjoy this book!.
Embrace the Season!.
Galatians 6:9

[signature]

ThisOneVoice@yahoo.com

SEASONS

OF THE

Soul

TERENCE SIKORYAK

BALBOA.PRESS

A DIVISION OF HAY HOUSE

Balboa Press books may be ordered through booksellers or by contacting:

Balboa Press
A Division of Hay House
1663 Liberty Drive
Bloomington, IN 47403
www.balboapress.com
844-682-1282

Scripture quotations marked NIV are taken from The Holy Bible, New International Version®, NIV® Copyright © 1973, 1978, 1984, 2011 by Biblica, Inc.® Used by permission. All rights reserved worldwide.

Scripture quotations marked ESV taken from The Holy Bible, English Standard Version® (ESV®), Copyright © 2001 by Crossway, a publishing ministry of Good News Publishers. All rights reserved.

Scripture quotations marked NASB are taken from The New American Standard Bible®, Copyright © 1960, 1962, 1963, 1968, 1971, 1972, 1973, 1975, 1977, 1995 by The Lockman Foundation. Used by permission.

Scripture quotations marked KJ21 are taken from the 21st Century King James Version®, copyright © 1994. Used by permission of Deuel Enterprises, Inc., Gary, SD 57237. All rights reserved.

Scripture quotations marked ASB/ASV are taken from the American Standard Version.

Scripture quotations marked KJV are taken from the King James Version.

Print information available on the last page.

ISBN: 978-1-9822-4568-9 (sc)
ISBN: 978-1-9822-4573-3 (e)

Balboa Press rev. date: 03/12/2021

I dedicate this book to my granddaughters; Lily, Ava, Aria and Carly. You are the newest Season of my Soul.

Contents

Seasons

I live in a place where the seasons change. It's where I choose to live. That's because there is something romantic about seasonal change. I can't explain it, but people who live here understand. In southern New Jersey, none of the seasons are very severe. It never gets unbearably cold in the winter, and it rarely gets to 100 degrees in the summer. We probably have less than twenty intolerable days in a year. But, the seasons change regularly. It is a system of constant and predictable change.

That is divinely ordered.

"As long as the earth lasts there will always be a time to plant and a time to gather. As long as the earth lasts there will always be cold and heat; there will always be summer, and winter, day and night." Genesis 8:22 NIV

Each season has it's own attributes, beauty and traditions, and every season has it's own work. Every season has its splender, and every season has it's danger. To neglect these truths is folly.

We go through seasons in our souls too. The souls can go through winter, where it is cold and dark and unfruitful. Some winters are more severe than others. It's what Saint John of the Cross described as the Dark Night of the Soul. It can be lonely and bitter. It can be depressing, and it can freeze your faith. No one is immune to this winter.

Walt Wilkins, in his song Long Winter
describes this dark cold time:

It was a long winter...spring sure took her sweet time
It was a long Winter...and I almost lost my mind
I felt like my prayers were frozen in midair
Stuck somewhere in the clouds
It was a long winter...but we're alright now

However, as Jim Rohn wrote, the spring always
follows the winter. How often? Every year! That truth
is what encourages us through the dark winter.

Spring

This is a collection of short devotions from my radio show "This One Voice". I am starting in the spring because that is when every thing comes to life. That's when I came to life. In 1977, I was living in California, and a number of people whom I worked with were sharing the Gospel with me. I grew up Catholic, so I had some awareness, but not what they were talking about. "Are you born again?", they would ask. That was foreign to me.

But in the spring of 1977, right around Easter, I accepted the Lord. I remember reading the Waste Land by T. S. Elliot in my English class, and thinking, "This is what is happening to me" Things that were dormant in my soul were coming to life, and some of it was disconcerting.

"April is the cruelest month, breeding
Lilacs out of the dead land, mixing
Memory and desire, stirring
Dull roots with spring rain.
Winter kept us warm, covering
Earth in forgetful snow, feeding
A little life with dried tubers."

Spring is a time of renewal and opportunity:

For behold, the winter is past;
The rain is over and gone.
The flowers appear on the earth,

The time of singing has come,
And the voice of the turtledove is heard in our land.
Song of Solomon 2:11-12 ESV

We don't build a significant life by coasting. If you
want to reap a life of fulfillment and happiness
you have to sow seeds of spiritual purpose.

Peter Drucker once wrote:
"The only things that evolve by themselves are
disorder, friction and malperformance."

Every day since May of 1977, I have read something
in or about the Bible. It was during a long winter
of my life when I drew upon all that I had sown.
And let me tell you, that relationship with God
that I had developed was almost not enough.

I believe that it was Joe Frazier who said: "Champions are
not made in the ring, they are only recognized there."

That means long hours of sowing those seeds of diligence. The
lesson of the spring is that as we sow, so shall we shall reap.

You can understand that, right?

Spring Training

Spring training is a time for hope!

Every fan has a fresh new outlook on their team. It's a new season, a clean slate, and everyone has a chance.

Sure, there are favorites going into every season. But every fan knows that anything can happen. And that's why we get excited about opening day. It's a new lease on life. I love spring training. Baseball season is right around the corner. My team, the San Francisco Giants, have a new beginning.

Wouldn't it be great if life were like that?

Wouldn't you get excited about a new beginning?

Well, the Apostle Paul says "Therefore if anyone is in Christ, they are a new creature; the old things have passed away; behold, new things have come. Now all things are from God, who reconciled us to Himself through Christ and gave us the ministry of reconciliation" 2Corinthians 5:17-18 NASB

That sounds great doesn't it?

You can be a new creation with a new heart, and a new nature. Life in the Spirit means a whole new season. It's a significant breakthrough in the destination of your life.

Richard Hamming wrote that any significant breakthrough for something new means a courageous break with the past. It requires "escape velocity."

Escape velocity is the power it takes to break the pull of the earth's gravitational pull. It takes momentum.

The Holy Spirit provides that momentum, that escape velocity to break the pull of the past.

A new season...A new beginning...And exciting future.

Pulling Weeds

There is an old Spanish Proverb ……. "There are more things that grow in the garden than the gardener sows" Anybody who has ever attempted a garden anywhere can appreciate that…there is one common enemy to all of us….

Weeds

No one makes room for weeds, they just show up.

It is a continuous work to rid your garden of weeds, because if you let them go, they will overrun the garden and choke the harvest. Sometimes you have to dig deep to get them out.

The same goes for our lives. There are things that crop up that we never planned to happen, There are directions that our lives take that we never intended when we set out. Jesus warned that the affairs and concerns of this life can choke the very breath from your soul.

What are the weeds in your life?

For some of us it's bitterness and anger. We tend to hold on to some of those things that choke our souls. And weeds don't just go away. Now, remember, no gardener in his right mind reserves room for weeds, don't let those things rob you of the joy that God promised.

<u>Here's what you do</u>
<u>Recognize</u> the things that are choking your soul.
<u>Determine</u> that you are going to remove these
things. Weeds never produce fruit.
<u>Pray for strength</u>. Best way to pull weeds is on your
knees anyway. God is willing and able to help.
<u>RECOGNITION</u>. <u>DETERMINATION</u>. <u>PRAYER</u>
This is weed control for your the soul…..

The Harvest is a joyful abundant Life.

Measure Twice, Cut Once

My friend Jim is a carpenter. As far as I can tell, he is
a pretty good one too. Recently Jim helped me with a
project at my house. One thing I observed by watching
Jim is that he follows the carpenter's rule to a tee.
Measure twice, cut once.
If you make sure the measurements are right before you
cut you avoid a whole lot of trouble down the road.
Measure twice, cut once.

That's a pretty good rule for any part of your life.
Just look at what you say. If we just measured what we
were going to say before we said it we would probably
avoid a whole lot of problems. The Bible says "A soft
word turns away anger" Prov. 15:1 ESV, but how many
times do we answer a bitter remark with a soft word?

And how about measuring actions. We ought
to know by now that everything we do has
consequences. Some good, Some bad.

The principles of carpentry probably haven't changed all
that much in the past 2,000 years: I mean nobody says
"Hey, this is a new century, we don't have to measure that
closely, precision isn't all that important today, would you
want anyone with that attitude building your house?"

And yet we build our lives on that attitude.

You see, I don't think that the principles for a solid character have changed all that much either. This may be the twenty-first century but what are the standards you look for when measuring someone's character? What standards do you use in your life? Is it what's acceptable in society...that changes from year to year...how do you keep track? Or do you use God's standard? Now that is the hard way - In the Book of Deuteronomy, God promises to bless every aspect of our lives if we just do it His way.

Measure that twice

The Final Authority

Babe Ruth was more than a great baseball player.
He was also a pretty colorful character, known
for his legendary antics on and off the field.

Legend goes, that one time when Ruth was
called out on strikes he gave a long hard look
at the umpire and said, "That was a ball"

"It was a strike" the umpire answered.

"It was a ball" Ruth said, "I know it, and there are
20,000 people in the stands who agree with me"

"That may be so," said the umpire "but
I'm the only one that counts"

Babe Ruth was out because the final authority had made
the call. No amount of arguing was going to change that.

Some day we will all face the ultimate authority; God. You
know the old saying "**nobody gets out of here alive**". At that
time what is going to be the call on your life? Assuming there
is a God, isn't also safe to assume he requires something of us?
Don't you think you should find that out? Aren't you curious?

Are you living a life that is pleasing to God?

No amount of protest will save you in the end, you have to make your plans on where you are going to spend eternity now.

What is God's call on your life......after all, <u>His is the only one that counts.</u>

When is a Good Thing a Bad Thing

When is a good thing a bad thing?

I know that that sounds like a riddle or some kind
of trick question, but it really does make sense.
And it's a good question to ask yourself.

When is a good thing a bad thing?

One day two sisters, Mary and Martha, had invited
Jesus to their house. Sometime during the visit Martha
noticed that she was doing all of the work while Mary
was in the other room sitting. She wasn't sitting watching
a football game, she was sitting at the feet of Jesus.
Martha, under the impression that she is being dumped on,
complains to Jesus "Lord don't you care…that my sister has
left me to do all of the work myself, tell her to help me!"
Jesus answers her "Martha, Martha you are troubled by so
many things, but only one thing is needed. Mary has chosen
what is better, and it will not be taken away from her."
A.W Tozer wrote *"..more spiritual progress can be made in one
short moment of speechless silence in the awesome presence of
God than in years of study. … When prostrate and wordless, the
soul receives divine knowledge like the flash of light on sensitive
film, exposure may be brief, but the results are permanent."*

**What is the story with Martha?
Is she trying to serve the Lord, or impress Him?**

I think that sometimes we try to impress
God with what we can do for Him...
and we do a lot of <u>Good</u> things.

But what God really wants most of all...
is to impress his image on us.

When is a good thing a bad thing?
When it takes the place of the best.

Mary had chosen the best, and as Jesus said,
it would not be taken away from her.

Ash Heap

A number of years ago I read a paper by Francis Schaeffer entitled *Ash Heap Lives.* The main idea of the paper is that most people spend all their time and money on things that are going to end up in a <u>garbage dump</u> or an <u>ash heap.</u>

He writes that *"… five minutes after we die our most treasured possessions which are invested in this life are absolutely robbed from us."*

Actually, What Schaeffer is saying is that we have become so wrapped up in this life that we have failed to make any provisions for the next.

The Apostle Paul writes in his first letter to the Corinthians that all believers in Christ will someday have their works judged by fire. Some will have works of gold silver and precious stones and others will have works of wood, hay, and stubble.

Well it doesn't take a genius to know that wood hay and stubble don't hold up to fire very well. What you are left with is an *Ash Heap.*

I don't know about you, but I don't want my life to add up to a big old *Ash Heap.* I want my life to have significance. Lasting significance. I want my life to touch people, especially those in my family, for generations after I am gone. But, I also want my life to have eternal significance. I don't want my life to add up to a big old ash heap.

Because you know what happens to an ash heap come the first small wind…It just blows away.

Shower Time

When he was young, my son Josh never used to like taking showers. It was a constant struggle in our house to get him to take one. One night, I was battling with him when he said" All right I'll take a shower, but I'm not going to wash!!" Sounds obstinate doesn't it?

As ridiculous as that sounds it is the way some people approach God. "I'll go to church, I'll sing the Hymns, and even stay awake during the message, But I'm not going to change. This is the way I am, and I will always be this way."

Sounds Obstinate doesn't it?

Jesus called the religious leaders of His time hypocrites. They put on a good appearance he said, but inside they were "full of robbery and wickedness" Luke 11:39 NASB

In God's eyes that is more than comical, it is Grotesque.

Spring is the season when many folks observe the tradition of Lent. The intention of Lent is to practice sacrifice and self-denial. Not because we want other people to see how religious we can be, or that we think that we can impress God, but because we want to, in some way, demonstrate how profoundly touched we are by His sacrifice.

The observance of Lent goes back to the Early Church Fathers. It is an opportunity to examine yourself, to understand the Crucifixion, and to give thanks for the Resurrection.

But going through the rituals of Christianity without coming away with a changed heart is a lot like taking a shower without washing.

You put on a good show, but you still stink.

Subway Schedule

My wife Jennifer and I spent a weekend in New York City. I love the city. But, as my mother used to say, nothing seems more ridiculous to me than the NYC subway schedule.

They're posted all over the place, and even if you could read them through the graffiti, it wouldn't take you very long to realize that nothing is on schedule. It's as if the city said "Well we have a train system, we really should have a schedule". But nobody really pays attention to it. Trains come when they come and that's the way it is. The schedule has become more or less window dressing.

Some people look at the Bible that way. It's as if people have decided that "the Bible has no relevance for today." And yet today, as we have come to the twenty-first century, the Bible has tremendous relevance.

The Bible is a realistic book. It reveals the meaning of our existence, and the origin of the universe. It is a marriage counselor, a child psychologist, and a business primer. It has challenged me to view life with a new perspective. It has comforted me in times of great distress.

The Bible declares that God is concerned with mankind in general, and every individual specifically. **Did you know that God is intimately concerned with you. He cares about your** fears and your problems. He has seen every single tear that you have cried, and he wishes the best for your life.

God is poised and eager to reveal himself to you, but you must seek Him.

You'll find Him in the Bible.

Best Friends

My oldest and closest friends are Brian Hamilton and
Kenny Henderson. We grew up around the block from
each other on Long Island. We went through school
together and played in a rock-n-roll band in high school.

Brian is the Godfather for one of my children and likewise, I
am the Godfather for one of his children. Together, we have
shared our best times and we have supported each other in the
worst of times. Over the years, though we have disappointed
each other more than a few times, yet we remain friends.

That is pretty much what friendship is all about isn't it?

**The Bible says that there is a friend that
"...sticks closer than a brother."**
Prov 18:24 (NIV)

That's the kind of friend that overlooks all of your
shortcomings, your bad moods, and your bad hair.

That's the kind of friend that suffers with you in hard times.
That's the kind of friend that genuinely rejoices
for you in your times of prosperity.

That's the kind of friend that esteems others more than
themselves and forfeits self-interest on your behalf.

I don't know if you have a friend like
that, but you could be one.
You could be a friend like that...

Would you be willing to set aside your pride
in order to bless a friend?
Would you be willing to carry the cross of blame
even when you are right?

That's a tall order...
But that's what Jesus did for us.
**And, those are the distinguishing features
of all of those who would call Him ... friend.**

Making Pancakes

Spring is a season when a lot of couples get married.
It can be a beautiful time for a wedding.

A friend of mine was reading to me a passage from a book
on marriage relationships. It sounded pretty syrupy so I
asked who the author was, I didn't recognize his name, but
she told me that he used to be married to this woman who
also writes books on relationships. As it turns out between
the two of them they have been married and divorced
6 times. They certainly have had lots of relationships,
but that doesn't necessarily make them experts. I have
had lots of colds, but that doesn't make me a doctor.

**I think it's funny that these two people sell so many
books...there sure are a lot of people taking their advice.**

**The Bible has advice for married couples too. It's
not very syrupy though. In fact, in most cases I
would say that it's pretty hard to swallow.**

Take for instance the advise for us husbands in Ephesians
chapter 5. The Apostle Paul says that husbands should
love their wives as Christ loves the church.... and gave
His life for it. **That means that we husbands should be
looking for ways to bless and serve our wives. Since
Christ came to be a servant not to be served.**

Now, I can't imagine that this would be very popular advice. I don't know about you, but I don't really want to be a servant at home. I don't necessarily want to be a king, but at least a benevolent dictator. Servanthood is a hard, hard road, and not at all syrupy.

And as my buddy Denny says "Everybody wants syrup, but nobody wants to make the pancakes."

Spotting Forgery

In my last semester in college I took a class on Art history. I went all around NYC to different galleries to view exhibits. It was a great adventure in the spring of 1982.

One of the most interesting things was art forgery. People could copy a painting by one of the masters in a way that is virtually undetectable to most people. In fact, there are only a few people who can detect these phony paintings. They know the artist so well that it almost impossible to fool them. Sometimes the smallest detail is the tip off. But even with their expertise sometimes a fake slips through, and it could cost the buyer millions of dollars.

Jesus said that we have to beware of frauds in the church too. Some of these frauds have been around for a long time-The Apostles fought them in the first century. Some of them are new, and we need to be able to detect them today.

Losing millions of dollars because of a fake is a terrible thing, but losing your soul because of a lie is a real tragedy.

There is really only one way to defend yourself from a lie. That is to become totally familiar with the truth. The Apostle Paul warned the Galatian church not to listen to any other Gospel. In fact, he says that if even an Angel comes and tells a different Gospel. Let him be accursed.

Now no one would buy an expensive painting without a qualified appraisal. How do you appraise the things that you believe? The Holy Spirit has a qualified eye for authenticity. Pray that the He leads you to the truth, and become familiar with the Bible.

Sometimes the smallest detail is the tip off.

Listening with New Ears

Not many people would recognize the name
Malchus. He is an important character in a classic
confrontation. A confrontation fueled by jealousy
and deceit, and carried out through betrayal.

You See, Malchus was the slave of the High priest
in Jerusalem. He was there the night when Jesus
was arrested, and he had the dubious distinction
of getting his ear cut off. (John 18:10)

During the confusion of the moment Peter draws his sword
to defend Jesus and poor Malchus receives the blow. But
in that moment, that moment of betrayal, that moment of
His arrest, Jesus tells Peter to put away his sword, and
then, out of compassion for this slave, He reaches out and
heals Malchus' ear. And in that moment Malchus moves
from devastation to restoration through a touch of Jesus.

You have to wonder what ever happened to that guy. He
is miraculously healed, so now does he go on with life
as usual. One might suspect that he was dramatically
changed. We never hear about him again though.

So What about you?

Has God ever worked a miracle in your life?

Has God ever touched you?

If so where does He find you years down the road?

**Still serving your old master, or listening
to a new Master with new ears.**

A Bag of Rocks

A few years ago, friends of mine went to Israel. I asked
them to bring me some mementos and they brought
me home a bag of rocks. They picked rocks from some
historical sites, labeled them and put them all in a
big plastic bag. Two of the most notable rocks were
from the Mount of Transfiguration and Calvary.

Now, over the years the labels have come off and the
rocks are all mixed up. But the rocks themselves are not
important it's the places they came from. These are two
mountains that mark significant events in the life of Christ,
and each event is mutually dependent on the other.

At the mount of Transfiguration, Jesus gives a select few
of His disciples a sneak preview of His glory. (Matt 17:1-3
NIV) But the glory revealed at the Mount of Transfiguration
would never come without the crucifixion at Calvary.
And the crucifixion is a meaningless act of suffering and
death if not for the Resurrection and Ascension to glory.

Now most of us would like to have that Mount of
Transfiguration experience…a glorious transformation
in our lives. But we all need our Calvary's. And
the man who picks up the cross is going down
that road alone, and he's not coming back.

**But change, real change, comes through
that cross. Otherwise, you're just another
indiscernible stone in a bag of rocks.**

Fame can be Fleeting

During the Easter Season, we mark the remembrance of The Lord's triumphal entry into Jerusalem. **Palm Sunday.**

People were celebrating the coming of their Messiah as He rode in on a donkey and they spread their clothes and lay down palms in the road.

"Hosanna to the Son of David;" they shouted, **"Blessed is he who comes in the name of the Lord; Hosanna in the Highest"** *Matthew 21:9 NIV*

But fame is fleeting isn't it?

You see, the same folks who were praising Him and laying palms at His feet on Sunday would be calling for His crucifixion on Friday.

<u>**There are some good lessons here for us.**</u>

<u>**Beware of the crowd.**</u> As Shakespeare warned, we tend to write men's faults in brass, and their virtues in water. How quickly the praise and adoration dissipate. The world is fickle.

<u>**What is the nature of your faithfulness?**</u>
Do you sing hosannas in church on Sunday, and deny Him the rest of the week?

Those of us who wish to sign-on as one of His disciples should heed the warning **"Don't be too easily converted"**

Because the road that leads into Jerusalem on Sunday morning also leads to Calvary on Friday afternoon.

Peter's Denial

Anybody who has ever heard the Gospel, knows
the account of Peter's denial of Jesus.

At the Last Supper, Jesus foretold it,
**"This night before the rooster crows you will
disown me three times"** *Matt26:34 NIV*

Later that night, after Jesus is arrested, Peter is in
the courtyard of the High priest, warming himself
by the fire, and someone recognizes him
**"You also were with Jesus the
Galilean"** Matt 26:69 (NKJV)

And even though Peter denies Him we really
can't be too hard on him. He had already come
farther than most of the other disciples.

Just this night he drew his sword to defend Jesus
from the Temple guards. He followed along to
the courtyard. He didn't turn and run.

But he hadn't gone far enough yet.

How many of us do the same?

We pledge our allegiance to God on Sunday morning, but
on Monday we warm ourselves by the worlds fires. We
don't want to stand out, we don't want to be recognized.

Just like Peter, we know too much to turn and run.

But that's not the end – Peter would do miraculous things for Him, and He **would** die for Him.

And God hasn't given up on you either. Even if you've denied Him. God hasn't given up on you!

**It's not too late.
You could change the world!**

From Pagan to Paschal

In the springtime we celebrate Easter Sunday. Now, the word Easter comes from the Old English word *eastron*. It was the name of an old pagan spring festival, called after Austro, a goddess of spring. One might wonder how a Christian high holy day got its name from a pagan festival. The answer is twofold.

It is the natural consequence of language in transition. It is another illustration of the power of God's grace, and the heart of the Easter message.

Around The 5th century, England was Christianized, and that conversion had far reaching linguistic changes. The changes came about in three different ways: foreign words were borrowed, new words were formed, and old words were changed. Because the existing language was not equipped to handle these new Christian ideas words like Easter shifted in meaning, and it came to be known as a holy Christian season.

The idea that something representing pagan religious practices could be used to denote a Christian holy day is unthinkable to some, but it's pretty typical of the way God works.

You see, at one time, my life was an affront to God. The thought that God would redeem this profane and faithless heart might be preposterous to some. The fact that God would use the torture and shame of the cross to accomplish

His greatest feat of mercy might seem preposterous to some. The fact that God would allow a convicted thief to escort His son into heaven might seem preposterous to some.

You see, God is able to take something pagan, something totally debased, and change it to something Holy. And that is the heart of the Easter message.

A Common Thread

Before Jesus left His disciples He promised to send
them a Paraclete, a comforter, The Holy Spirit.

It is through the Holy Spirit that our minds would be opened
to Divine truths. We are personally, and intimately led into the
depths of God. We no longer rely on our own finite reasoning.

It is through the Holy Spirit that we would
encounter God's gift of peace. We would no
longer be subject to our own emotions.

It is through the Holy Spirit that God confers on us
an indelible seal of faith. This magnificent seal would
bind us to every Christian who has ever lived before
us, and every Christian who will live after us.

This is an incomprehensible reality.

This is so deep and so far reaching that it boggles the mind
that there is such division, and bitterness amongst Christians.
That could only be the result of our own selfish pride.

Jesus left us with more than a new religious
thought. He gave us a common thread that weaves
through all of history and into eternity.

Fielders and Fig Trees

In the 1980's the Phillies drafted a young second baseman, who they thought showed great potential. Through the next few years he would prove to be a good player, but he never lived up to that potential. Eventually the Phillies got tired of waiting, so they traded him away. Since then he has been on a number of different teams, each one thinking he showed great potential, each one, in the end, disappointed.

You see, in major league baseball there is no room for unrealized potential. If you can't produce:

YOU GO!

In the parable of the barren fig tree, Jesus tells of a landowner who wants to cut down an unproductive tree. "Look, for three years I have come looking for fruit on this fig tree without finding any", he says, "Cut it down, why waste good ground" *Luke 13:7 NIV*

"Leave it alone", pleads the keeper "I'll work on it, give it some special attention for a year. If then it doesn't produce, then cut it down." *Luke 13:8 KJV (paraphrase)*

Apparently there is no room in groves for unproductive trees.

But is that what Jesus is telling us? Is he giving us a lesson on Agriculture? Or is He telling us something about God's Kingdom?

Would Jesus take the time to give such a strong
teaching if nothing was ever required of us?

Ask Yourself:

**Am I a fruit producing person in God's Kingdom?
Am I living up to my potential, Using
my gifts and talents for Him?**

Or am I just taking up space?

Discipline and Regret

Years ago I learned that there are two pains in life

"The pain of discipline or the pain of regret"

And if you won't endure the pain of discipline
you will always have the pain of regret.

Discipline is the strength of character that resolves to
go on long after the original enthusiasm has waned.
It's that energy that picks us up over and over again.
Unfortunately, it is not a thing that many people pursue.
But happiness, real happiness will never be realized
until discipline and perseverance are developed.

When my son Jaimie was going for his black belt he
wanted to quit a few times. I encouraged him to keep
going. "Think about the day you will wear that black belt.
You will know how you earned it. You paid the price."

Jesus warned his disciples to count the cost of following Him.

**"No one would build a tower", He tells them "Without
first counting the cost. Otherwise when he has laid the
foundation and is not able to finish, all who observe it will
begin to ridicule him." (Luke 14:28 paraphrase NIV)**

I see a lot of unfinished business out there. Folks who
never considered the whole cost when they set out. I see it
in marriages, businesses, I see it a lot in Christianity. You

see, it takes more than inspiration to follow through with things… It takes discipline, and discipline is hard work.

Sam Ewing once said "Hard work spotlights the character of people. Some turn up their sleeves, some turn up their noses, and some, well some don't turn up at all."

Jaimie did get his black belt. In fact he and his brother Josh continued to become third degree black belts. They paid the price.

The Prodigal Brother

Most people are familiar with the parable of the Prodigal Son. A boy cashes in his inheritance, and leaves his father's home to make it on his own. Eventually, when his pockets are empty and so is his stomach he lands a job feeding hogs. It's there in the pig pen that he realizes:

"Even the servants in my father's house have it better than this. I will humble myself, and maybe my father will take me back as a servant." *Luke 15:17 NIV paraphrase*

Now, There are two different reactions to the boy's return. The father, as you would expect is overjoyed, and he throws a party in honor of his returning son. The older brother though doesn't share his father's feelings. He is angry.

But we shouldn't be too hard on this guy. Look, he's served the father faithfully. He's worked the family business day in and day out while his little brother was out whooping it up. We can understand why he might have some resentment. But he doesn't know his father's heart.

You know, a lot of people feel that God is angry at them. That even if they did go back to Him maybe He wouldn't want them.

Unfortunately that's because they've met too many big brothers, but you see that's not the heart of the father. Jesus told His disciples that all of heaven rejoices at the repenting of one soul.

If you haven't been to church for a while not everyone will be overjoyed to see you there.

But I will guarantee you, that the only One who counts will be happy to see you there.

Summer

Summer is a tough season. It is the time for vacation, swimming at the pool and beach time. But it can be challenging. Summer is a time for greater vigilance.

Depending on where you live, the summer months can be very oppressive. It is hot and it is humid. Even in the desert where there is no humidity, the temperature can get up as high as 120. In the summer, I have to work hard in my garden, All sorts of weeds and bugs show up. I find snakes in the weeds in my garden too.

Summer is also a time for the beach,. I grew up on Long Island. And I remember my mom taking us to Jones' Beach. Then, as a teenager, we would hitch-hike there. In my twenties, I lived in California, not far from the beach and now I live in Ocean City, NJ, only blocks from the beach. We spend a lot of time at the beach.

It gets really crowded in Ocean City in the summer. People plan all year to come here for a week or two. People sacrifice all year to spend time in the town where I live all year round.

I think that's pretty cool!

Summer is when I get to ride my bike the most. I love it! But summer brings some dog days too. You have to persevere.

"For day and night your hand was heavy upon me; my strength was sapped as in the heat of the summer." Psalm 32:4 NIV

If we plant in the spring but we neglect to water and protect in the summer, we will end up with nothing much in the fall. These are the dry times in life. We must be diligent.

Have you ever gotten down in the garden in the summer? There is all sorts of crud there. I find weeds, spiders and one time, I found this unrecognizable frog.

But, if we neglect the garden in the summer:

"I went past the field of the sluggard, past the vineyard of someone who has no sense; thorns had come up everywhere, the ground was covered with weeds, and the stone wall was in ruins. I applied my heart to what I saw; A little sleep, a little slumber, and a little folding of the hands to rest, and poverty will come on you like a thief, and scarcity like an armed man." Proverbs 24:30-32 NIV

We need to protect because there are more things that grow in the garden than the gardener plants.

Sometimes we have to weed out toxic people in our lives...they can choke our souls and hinder our growth. Summer is a time when we exercise self control. It's easy to do nothing...but the crops will get run over.

Our hearts naturally drift toward comfort. But, I like what the Marines say about comfort:

"Comfort is an illusion. A false security, bred from familiar things and familiar ways. It narrows the mind and weakens the body and robs the soul of spirit and determination"

Summer is a time when we work through discomfort, and work though we see no results. But, like the song by David Wilcox:" All the Roots Grow Deeper When its Dry"

We are going to need those deeper
roots when the winter comes.

Memorial Day

Memorial Day is the kick-off for Summer. It is
not technically summer, but where I live, at the
Jersey Shore, it is the beginning of summer.

Memorial day was originally observed on May 30, 1868,
Instituted on the order of General John Alexander Logan, for
the purpose of decorating the graves of American Civil War
dead. Today we honor the memory of all service personnel
killed in wartime. It is a day when we commemorate those
men and women who paid the ultimate price for our freedom.

Lately, it's become a day for family get-togethers, and
barbecues. Many towns do take the time to make this
day a big event with parades, speeches, and concerts
in the park. We do all of this in hope that someday our
children will ask, **"What is this all about?"** We should
take that opportunity to impress upon them the price
that was paid for the freedom that they enjoy today.
No generation should ever take that for granted.

In the Christian faith we have a Memorial Day of
sorts. The tradition is about 2000 years old. It's any
day that we celebrate Communion. Jesus originally
instituted it at the last Supper. He told His disciples
**"As often as you do this (eat the bread) - do it in
Remembrance of Me" 1 Cor. 11:23-25 NIV (Paraphrase)**

In the communion we proclaim the Passion and Death of
Christ. It is both a Mournful and Joyful proclamation.

It is Mournful because our sinfulness made the crucifixion necessary. You see the crucifixion didn't only save people in the first Century, it was for you and I today too. We should always be mindful of the terrible price paid for our Redemption. **Grace is a free gift, but it's not cheap.**

It's also a joyful commemoration. You see, anyone who receives that Gift of Salvation will be acceptable to God.

Communion is also our visual sermon. When we eat the Bread and drink the Wine we honor the Lord and we remember the ultimate price paid for us. And Hopefully, our children will ask us:

"What is this all about?"

And we can explain that our faith not only looks back on the promises God has fulfilled, but we also look forward to the promise That Jesus Gave "Yes, I am coming soon."

Ladders and Walls

🌿

Stephen Covey once pointed out that too many of **us spend our whole lives climbing the ladder of success one rung at a time, only to find in the end, that the ladder is leaning against the wrong wall.**

I've spent a lot of time leaning that ladder against the wrong wall. Trying to impress people by how religious I could act or speak. That was exhausting though. Not because I didn't know how to act or what to say, but because I simply couldn't keep it up. Besides, I was expending all my energy trying to please men instead of living of life pleasing to God.

Jesus once told the religious leaders **"You are those who justify yourselves in the sight of men, but God knows your hearts; for that which is highly esteemed among men is detestable in the sight of God"** Luke 16:15 (ESV)

I'd say that detestable is a pretty strong word. And it is interesting that the only time Jesus ever uses it is to describe the most religious people of His time. He's not saying that religious people are detestable. Just that some of their motives are, or at least some of the things that they esteem most highly.

Many of us climb the ladder of success pursuing those things that men esteem most highly.

47

How far up that ladder are you willing to go before
you change your heart. You can fool everyone else
for just so long, and when you slip up most of them
will move on to the next great religious hero.

But as long as your heart is pure, God will never move on.

God Will Never Move On.

All Consuming Sin

On His way to Jerusalem, where He will soon be arrested and crucified, Jesus stops to heal 10 men stricken with leprosy. Now, leprosy is a bacteria that attacks the nerves and muscles resulting in disfigurement, loss of extremities, and ultimately death. It is a putrid disease.

And curiously enough, after having been delivered from this horrible disease, that will certainly consume their lives, only one returns to give thanks.

The fact that only one returns does not slip Jesus' attention. **"Were there not ten cleansed?" he asked "Where are the other 9"** Luke 17:17 NIV

I guess you could say that 9 out of 10 lepers will not show appreciation for God's miraculous healing.

And 2,000 years later what percentage of us show thanks to God for His mercies in our lives.

Do we just go on our way with an air of arrogance? Somehow convincing ourselves that we merit God's favor. You see, ingratitude is a putrid condition.

I don't want to be like that anymore, I want to be like that one guy. The guy who goes back.

I want to be reminded every day that…

Were it not for the mercies of God. My sins would have consumed me.
Lam 3:22 NIV (paraphrase)

49

Chaos

My daughter Sarah loves summer storms.

When she was little she was terrified of thunderstorms, but when she was a teenager she would sit out on the porch and watch the lightening. When she got her driver's license, she would drive out to Seven Bridges Road to watch the storm over The Great Bay.

James Gleick is a professor of chaos theory. In his book, entitled "Chaos", he explains that all systems, such as waterfalls, and thunderstorms, can be represented by simple mathematical equations.

What he found in researching storm patterns was that storms may be mathematically predictable, but tiny differences in input, such as water temperature or even slight changes in wind, would result in overwhelmingly large differences in out put. The equation was radically altered.

This is more than an interesting mathematical sidebar though. I see encouraging implications for our lives. We could become dynamic instruments of change in our lives and the lives of those around us. We can change the input.

What would be a life changing input for us?

How about reading, and meditating on God's Word?

In Psalm 63, the Psalmist wrote, "I think of thee upon my bed, and meditate on thee in the watches of the night." *Psalm 63:6 NIV Paraphrase*

Do you think that would make a difference?
God's Word has a purifying effect, doesn't it?
Our faith does present us with some supernatural opportunities. Suppose you took a situation or a person in your life, and fasted and prayed over them.

Do think that would make a difference?

Professor Gleick's research shows us that the way things look to be going is not the way that they have to turn out.

If we even make slight changes to the input of our lives we can dramatically change the output.

Good Choices

Buckminster Fuller once wrote **"In every bad circumstance there are good choices."**

Those good choices are not always that easy to recognize though. Our tendency to react right away tends to cloud our judgment and in the heat of the moment we make bad decisions. I know that I am guilty of that in so many situations. We need to realize that:

"In every bad circumstance there are good choices"

The crux of the problem is that every situation does not require immediate response. Sometimes if you stop before you respond you can save a lot of trouble. You see, most of us are governed more by human emotions rather than the Love of God.

The Bible Says
"A soft answer turns away wrath" Proverbs 15:1 (ESV)

But a soft answer is not what immediately comes to my mind when someone is in my face. That's because the decision of how we are going to respond in all circumstances requires a decision of how to respond before the circumstance arises. I'm not talking about Positive Mental Attitude. I'm talking about making a commitment to portray the Wisdom and Love of Christ in all circumstances. **Responding in Wisdom and Love.** I don't know about you, but that is truly beyond my capacity. It takes supernatural grace that comes from the Holy Spirit.

I'm not talking about being a doormat either. I'm talking about developing a depth of character that is uniquely refreshing in today's "Me First" society. I'm talking about the imitation of Christ.

We can't control bad circumstances. We can't control other people's attitudes. We can control our choice of response though.

It takes a keen eye to find those good choices in bad circumstances.

No Plan – No Budget

Suppose someone offered to build you a house, and when you asked to see the blueprints they said:

"Oh we don't use blueprints, we just get a lot of good ideas as we go along. Besides, we don't like to stifle the creativity of our people. And of course we can't tell you how much it will cost. We'll just see what happens."

No plans…No budget.
Well, that may work for the government. But you wouldn't build a house that way. Unfortunately though, that's the way most people run their lives.
No Plan - No Budget

The Bible says,
**"A plan in the heart of a man is like deep water,
But a man of understanding draws it
out" Proverbs 20:5 NASB**

We make plans for lots of things. We plan weddings, we plan vacations. Pilots make flight plans. They may have to alter their course along the way, but they always have the destination clearly in mind.

What about life though? How many people draw out a flight plan for life? How many people sit down and ask themselves "What direction do I want my life to take? What is most important to me?"

The man of understanding has a clear vision built on solid foundations. Based on the tough questions of life. What type of person do I want to be? What type of husband/wife, father/mother, do I want to become?

The man of understanding knows the destination so the steps he takes are always in the right direction.

Someone once said of Bill Bright (the founder of Campus Crusade for Christ), that he didn't become successful by doing big things, but by doing a lot of little things in a singular direction.

You see, the man of understanding doesn't get distracted or discouraged by obstacles nor setbacks, he draws security and encouragement from his vision. Because the blueprint for his life is thought out and prayed over

He does a lot of little things in a singular direction.

A Win / Win Proposition

A lot of people look at Christianity as a win/lose proposition. God wins your soul and you give up almost everything you enjoy and lose most of your friends. To tell you the truth, if that actually was the deal I would still take it. But there is so much more to it.

Matthew Henry, a pastor in the 1600's, once wrote *"You may lose for God, but you will never lose by Him."*

Over 40 years ago when I became a Christian I gave up a lifestyle that was guaranteed to end in disaster. I also lost some friends too. But I lost friends when I went to college, I lost some friends when I moved to California, and then again when I moved back to the East Coast.

"You may lose for God, but you will never lose by Him"

I can testify, with all honesty, that anything that I have given up for the sake of God I have gained back tenfold. I must confess, that really I didn't lose anything.

You know, most people live their lives in quiet desperation. They run a race to find security and contentment in a bankrupt world. But God promises an abundant life of joy, peace, and contentment in this world and life forever with Him in the next.

I don't know about you, but to me that sounds like a win-win proposition.

Remember "You may lose for God, but you will never lose by Him"

Rules of the River

Pat Riley, in his book The Winner Within, tells a story about when he went white river rafting with some friends on the Colorado River. The guides on the trip took great pains to make sure that everyone knew and understood what they called the **Rules Of The River.**

Rule #1 is:
If you fall overboard you must be an active participant in your own rescue.

Too may times people will fall in the water and panic, making it all the more difficult to rescue them. Or they will leave all the work up to the guides. This also makes it difficult. So everyone has to know before they set out **If you fall overboard you must be an active participant in your own rescue.**

That is a rule that we should hand out every Sunday in Church. Too many people fall overboard and expect God to reel them back in or for the Church to send out rescue parties, and they do nothing. They refuse to be active participants in their own rescues.

Now the Bible has it's own **Rules of the River** if you would. Rule #1 I guess would be:

If you have fallen overboard you must repent.
You need to change the direction you are going and get back on board. You do that by:

Reading your Bible: It's more than knowing about God, but we can actually know God through the Bible and the Illumination of the Holy Spirit.

Praying: Nothing moves God into action like prayer. Jesus told us to Ask, to Seek, and to Knock. Those are action verbs. They make you an active participant.

Going to Church: Church gives us an opportunity to worship God as a group. Jesus said "Whenever two or more are gathered in My name I will be there." Church gives an opportunity to Serve too. "If you want to be great in the Kingdom of God learn to be a servant."

If you want to be an active participant in your own Spiritual life: Read the Bible, Pray, and Go to Church.

Constancy of Purpose

W. Edward Demings is the father of *Total Quality Management*. Anyone who has worked for a corporation in the past few decades would be familiar with *Total Quality Management*. Actually it is a theory of business management that has been popular in Japan for many years, but has only become respected in the US for the past few decades.

The theory basically focuses on

The foundation, says Deming, to a successful organization or even a successful individual is **CONSTANCY OF PURPOSE**.

"a strong, empowering, guiding, inspiring, and uplifting purpose"

The first commandment focuses in on that way of thinking; **"I am the Lord your God, You shall not have any other Gods before me" Exodus 20:2-3 ESV** The funny thing about a self made man, is that he tends to worship his creator.

Anything that you trust more than God in effect becomes your God. Some people put all their trust in riches and fame. Some people put all their trust in education.

You see, we all know what money, and what education can do for us and even what other people can do for us, but most of us are not too sure what God will do for us. Even though He says to put our trust in Him and let Him show what He can do.

Trusting in God is mentioned 116 times in the Bible:
Now that is **Constancy of Purpose.**
The author of the book of Psalms wrote "**I have set the Lord _always_ before me**" Psalm 16:8 (ESV)
and "**My eyes are _ever_ toward the Lord.**"
Psalm 25:15(ESV)
words like ever and always.

They represent <u>Constancy of Purpose.</u>

The Nice Dad

Having six children doesn't make me an authority on fatherhood. It should count for something though. Maybe I am just six times more frustrated than any one else. It is my hearts desire to be the best dad that I can be. I've read books on being a dad, listened to tapes, and watched videos. I am on a lifetime quest for being a successful DAD.

I wanted to see if the Bible has some advise on being a dad. What I found was: "**Fathers don't exasperate your children**" That's it. That's what the Apostle Paul has to say about being a father. In fact, he says it in two different letters "**Fathers don't exasperate your children.**" *Ephesians 6:4 NIV*

I may be on the wrong road here because everything I do seems to "**exasperate my children**". Or maybe my kids are easily exasperated. I've read about conditions like that, some sort of chemical imbalance. They probably get it from their mother's side too. I can't remember anyone in my family ever being a **Hyper- Exasperant.** But my friend is a nurse and she tells me there is no such ailment.

I must be an exasperating person.

Now the meaning of exasperate in the dictionary is *"to irritate or annoy very much; make angry; to vex"*

I hate to think about myself as an irritating and annoying person. I don't want to be vexing. And I'm just about convinced that I am when my son Josh gives me this poem that he wrote about me for Father's Day:

The Nice Dad
When I feel sad I got my Dad
He calms my fears and wipes away my tears
He tells a joke when I am down
and turns my frown upside down
He is great at hockey and scores lots of goals
He reads me the Bible and to help save my Soul
Of all the men God could send
He's not only my Dad, He's my friend.

Used by permission
You see, that's not what you write about an exasperating person. Maybe I am on the right track. And maybe I am right about my kids being Hyper-Exasperant.

If they are…. I know they probably get it from their mother's side.

Fifteen Minutes of Fame

Andy Warhol once said "In the future everyone will be famous for 15 minutes." I don't know how true that is, but we all have our special days. Days that are set aside for us alone like our birthdays, graduations, and weddings.

Usually we send out invitations far enough in advance to allow people to make plans to share these times with us. We ask, "Set this time aside" and "Please bless us with your presence"

God has sent out invitations too. He sent them out thousands of years ago. The invitation is in the Fourth Commandment. "Six days you will have to labor", he says "But the seventh belongs to Me, remember to keep this day Holy" *Exodus 20:9-10 NIV (paraphrase)*

God asks that we set aside our own priorities each week and worship Him.

A number of years ago my brother passed away. Because we knew that some people had to come a distance (a two hour drive, no big deal) we made arrangements so that some people would have ample time to be there to pay their respects. Much to my surprise, a number of my family members didn't show. They didn't even call. Whatever it was they were doing they couldn't put aside to pay their respects. I felt they owed my brother that much, they certainly owed my father.

I got a good taste of how God must feel. We make a lot of excuses why we don't go to church, (None of them any good.) God is not interested in your excuses anyway. I've even heard people say "Sunday is the only day I get to golf"

Let me ask you something.

Would you be so diligent to work on your golf game and yet neglect your soul?

Honor Your Parents

One out of every two marriages end in divorce. Single parent families have tripled in the past thirty-five years. The juvenile violent crime rate has risen by 300% since 1965, teen pregnancy has quadrupled, and suicide is the second leading of causes of death among teens, behind accidents. Does this sound like the great new society? The Brave New World?

This is the legacy of my generation. The baby boomers, the beat generation. We had a better way than our parents, we were more enlightened. We had a clear and concise message for our parents too.

Get out of the way, the Times they are a Changing.

The times sure have changed haven't they, but not for the better. You can blame only so much on TV and friends you know, but actually, when it comes right down to it my generation hasn't done a very good job. And yet in light of all that God's message to the youth of today is:

Honor your Parents

This is one of the toughest commandments for people, it always was for me…simply because a good many parents are not very honorable.

But it is something very dear to the heart of God. In fact, He has promised that if you will honor your parents that He will bless your life. I guess for those whose parents are especially hard to honor because of abuse and neglect will be given a better blessing. It hasn't slipped God's attention that you have been abused or abandoned, you can rest assured in that.

The Bible says that anyone who honors their parents lives a life that is pleasing in God's eyes.

Wouldn't you want to live a life Pleasing in the sight of God? … So now the next time you are angry at your parents, take the fifth. The fifth commandment that is;

Honor your parents……

The Value of a Soul

There is something special about Humans. Now, some scientists would debate that. They would have us believe that we are simply on a higher level of the evolutionary plain than other animals, and we are not all that different. But, come on…look around you, look at your cars, look at your cities, look at your radio…let's face it, we're different.

How else would you explain a young man tortured and twisted by cerebral palsy writing deep thought provoking and heart wrenching poetry. Or a man crippled by polio becoming a world class violinist. You see we humans possess more than just biological existence, it goes much deeper than that. Deep inside we have emotions, intellect and a will…

It's our Soul
Psychologists call it the ID the Personality the Psyche. It is the signature of God on His greatest creation. You see, all of nature portrays the magnificence of God, but nothing showcases His wonder better than the Human Soul.

That's why he puts such a high value on human life. "Thou shalt not Kill" is the sixth commandment *Ex 20:13 NIV*. There are terrible consequences when you break this commandment. When one man deliberately murders another, God told us, his life is then forfeited. Society must avenge the murder. That's not the same as revenge though, it's the administration of justice.

Somehow we have come to think of ourselves as more reasonable now "We are more compassionate" But who is more compassionate than God? Are we more compassionate than God? I think that everyone would agree that capital punishment doesn't make everything alright. It doesn't make everybody even. Is it a deterrent though? It wasn't established as a deterrent…It is a proclamation. It proclaims that we hold human life most precious. Because we have failed to do this we live in such violent times. We don't need to scare people, we need to establish in the hearts of men the proper value of human life.

The same value that God holds for it.

Contract vs. Covenant

**I was wondering ...What is the difference
between a contract and a covenant?**
I looked them up, and though the definitions are
close the true meanings are worlds apart.
A contract is an agreement, usually on paper signed, and
witnessed, and of course, reviewed and approved by lawyers.
(You can't be too careful.) Now it would seem with all
this writing and reviewing, signing and witnessing, that a
contract would be a binding agreement. But as much as men
try they just can't get each other to honor their contracts.

Now a covenant is something altogether different. It has to do
with sacred things. It is sealed by a vow. The binding factor of
a covenant is the character and integrity of the one making the
vow. Unlike a contract a covenant is not enforced by the laws
of men, it falls under the jurisdiction and authority of God. If
you think you should be careful about entering into a contract,
you should really be careful about the vows you make.

Take for instance Marriage. Marriage is a covenant.
When we get married we make a vow before God.
Now God is pretty serious about covenants. He keeps
the ones He makes, He expects us to keep ours.

"Thou shalt not commit Adultery" Ex 20:14 NIV
is the seventh commandment. It's repeated over and
over throughout the whole Bible. Over 50 times God
mentions the commandment or the consequences

for breaking it. God is serious about the Marriage vow. We don't take him too seriously anymore.

I was reading in a Christian men's magazine that 30% of the men that they polled admitted to committing adultery. These were men who professed to being Christians. We don't take God seriously anymore.

In every contract there is some sort of loophole. If you are clever enough you can break your word and the courts will back you up. That's not very principled, but it is legal.

There aren't any loopholes with God's commandments though. No subtle obscurities that can be twisted and reinterpreted to suit our fancy. Now, it all comes to this one question: **Do you take God seriously or not?**

Why do People Steal?

Willie Sutton was a bank robber in the 1940's. It took quite some time to catch him, and when they did the legend says that someone asked him "Willie, why do you rob banks?", "Because that's where the money is" he answered. That's a pretty witty answer, but it skirts the deeper meaning of the question. **Why do men rob banks?**

Why do teenagers kill other teenagers for a pair of sneakers? Is there something intrinsically magical about certain sneakers? Why does a highly educated and seemingly successful bank executive defraud hundreds of people out of their life savings bringing shame on his family and ruining the lives of all those who put their trust in him?

Why do we steal?

We all know that it's wrong. The eighth commandment says **"Thou shalt not steal"** Ex20:15 NIV But even beyond that, deep inside, people who don't even believe in God know that stealing is wrong.

Even thieves know it's wrong. That's why they so vehemently deny guilt. Nobody wants to be known as a low life feckless thief. And yet even though we all know that stealing is wrong we still make that decision to steal. **Why?**

It's probably because we're not convinced that the world is not the end all. **Get it while you can. You only live once.**

C.S. Lewis once wrote "Most people, if they really learned to look into their own hearts would know that they do want, and want acutely, something that cannot be had in this world. There are all sorts of things in this world that offer to give it to you, but they never quite keep their promise." Mere Christianity

They never keep their promise... those things that we set our hearts on. I guess it all comes down to contentment. What will it take to make you content? Is it material things?

If I could just have those sneakers, If I could only drive that car. The urge is enough to make some people go against their consciences and steal.

But you know. Deep in your heart ...
that if you drink from that well you will thirst again.

Bearing False Witness

A number of years ago I was at a summer family reunion when I overheard two people talking about me (I wasn't eavesdropping). It was just by virtue of where I was standing that I overheard what they were saying. And what they were saying about me was not very flattering. It was weird too, because it wasn't the sort of thing that I couldn't protest. It was how they felt about me, and they obviously had a low opinion of me.

It hurt though. Especially since the person that said it I had always held in high regard, and actually still do today. But since that day something had changed, I knew, in no uncertain terms, what they really thought about me. Something was taken away that day too.

Now the 9th commandment says "Thou
shalt not bear false witness"
Ex 20:16 NIV. But is that false witness? It's an opinion isn't it? I mean we are entitled to our opinions aren't we? What is bearing false witness any way? Is it just lying or is it something more?

Well, amongst other things it is:

**"Speaking unjustly against another person,
to the detriment of their reputation"**

But I've done that. I do it all the time. It's just the
truth right? And sometimes the truth hurts.
Well sometimes the truth does hurt, but it
doesn't have to be hurtful and malicious.

I ought to know better too. I've been on the other end
of that stinging truth deal myself. But what about
my opinion? Oh yeah my opinion. You know I've
convinced myself that there is a tremendous void in
the universe that can only be filled by my opinion.

**You see, the truth points in the right direction and builds
character. A false witness always takes our eyes off
God and tears down others. We ought to realize that if
we want to gain the respect of those present we need to
protect the reputation of those who are not present.**

Mom's Best Advice

The Sociologist Laurence Shames, wrote in his book, entitled "The Quest for More" about the rise of materialism in the 1980's. He writes that despite the tremendous material success of so many people there still was a prevailing emptiness. He says that:

"Personal disasters ranging from cocaine abuse to sundered marriages to alcoholism to suicide were ascribed not to the stresses of failure, or even the stresses seeking success, but rather the disillusionment that came with success itself."

"The disillusionment that came with success itself." That's an interesting consequence. We spend our whole lives looking at what other people have, convincing ourselves that if we could only have what they have, we could be happy too. Of course we are assuming that the people that we are envying are happy in the first place.

This is what the Bible calls covetousness. The tenth commandment says **"Thou shalt not covet your neighbors possessions"** don't covet their house, don't covet their husband or wife, or their ox or donkey. Don't covet anything that they own period.

One day my mother and I were out for a drive. She was telling me how much fun she had when me, my sister, and my brothers were young, she was relishing those memories. **"These are the best days of your life"** she said **"Enjoy your wife and your children, don't worry about money and things, cause in the**

end those things are not important." The next day my mother went into a coma, she never recovered.

Her last bit of advice was the best. Stop looking over the other guys fence. Stop looking in the other guys garage. Start enjoying what you have today.

I pray that you can find contentment in those things that God has blessed you with. I pray that you look on your husband or wife with an eagerness to Bless them. I think that it's possible for us to work towards a better tomorrow and still appreciate today!

The Wrong Road

I was on my way to an appointment one summer morning.
It was the first time I had gone to this place so I left with
plenty of time to spare just in case. Somewhere close to the
destination I realized that I had probably made a wrong turn.
And even though I had this deep down feeling that I was
going the wrong way… I sped up. Maybe out of anxiety I
sped up, but if I was in fact, going the wrong way, now I was
getting further away from my intended destination faster.

I was on the wrong road, but I was making great time.

As ridiculous as that sounds that's the way many of us
run our lives. Something deep inside tells us that we
are going the wrong way, but we convince ourselves
to keep going ahead "**Well, let me just go a little bit
further, let me just get around the bend here.**"

Until one day we find we're so far off course
and we are literally running out of time.

I could have stopped that morning, Checked my directions
and figured out where I went wrong and then corrected
myself, eventually I did. But every minute I drove in
the wrong direction I compounded my problem.

All of us have a destination and a timetable. We choose
the destination, but no one is sure of the timetable.
I guess since none of us knows how much time we
have being on the right road is critical, isn't it?

Jesus once said to His disciples "What would it profit a man to gain the whole world and lose his soul?" Mark 8:36 kjv

What does it profit us to speed up when we're going in the wrong direction?

Take the time to stop, read the directions, and correct mistakes.

You avoid a lot of pain...you avoid a lot of regrets.

Forgive and Forget

Next to Michael Jordan, Wayne Gretzky is probably the most recognized sports figure in America. "The Great One", as he has been nicknamed, has shattered records in hockey that have stood for decades. Throughout his career in the National Hockey League he has always kept his image clean avoiding controversy and trouble.

Someone asked Gretzky what is the secret to his success. **"I skate to where the puck is going", he said, "Not to where it's been"**

You see, Wayne Gretzky is actively involved in the play that is currently developing in front of him. Now for anyone who has ever seen a hockey game you know that there is always a lot of pushing and grabbing behind the play. This is usually initiated by players with less ability trying to distract the better players from being involved in the play in front of them.

How about you? Are you actively involved in the play in front of you or have you been suckered into dwelling on the anger and bitterness of the past.

The Bible teaches that there is a special blessing for those of us who will let go of the anger of the past. Every bit of bitterness that we carry over from yesterday reduces our effectiveness today.

Forgive and forget

How many times have you heard people say or maybe you have even said yourself "I will forgive, but I won't forget" Now what kind of forgiveness is that?

The essence of forgiveness is letting go and moving on. The book of Proverbs says **"It is the glory of a man to pass over a transgression"** Proverbs 19:11 ASV

How much room can there be for joy in your heart when it is filled with anger and bitterness. Let's take a lesson from Wayne Gretzky...Forgetting those negative things in our past and moving forward in our lives.

Sowing and Reaping

One of the most powerful lessons that we can learn
in life is the principle of sowing and reaping.

Basically what we are today is due to what we did
yesterday, and what we are tomorrow is largely
due to what we do today. There is no getting
around the principle of sowing and reaping.

The Apostle Paul wrote that if we sow to our evil
inclinations we will reap corruption in our lives.

The works of the evil deeds he says are:

**"…impure thoughts, eagerness for lustful pleasures,
idolatry, hatred and fighting, jealousy and anger, selfish
ambitions, dissensions, factions, envy, drunkenness, and
orgies and the like."** *Galatians 5:19-20 NASB Paraphrase*

This behavior will lead to corruption
in our lives on so many levels.

It corrupts our lives physically:
There are 40,000 new cases of sexually
transmitted diseases reported every day.
This year, 1 in 4 teens will contract a STD.
These diseases lead to hepatitis, liver cancer, cirrhosis,
cervical cancer and infertility to name a few.

When you sow to your evil inclinations...you reap corruption.

<u>It corrupts our lives emotionally:</u>
Fulton Sheen once wrote that too many people seek help
in therapy when what they really need is a confessor.

How many marriages are ruined by evil inclinations? Look
at the list! How many of these behaviors do you display?

How many relationships have we ruined
because of our evil inclinations?

Fall

I would say that fall is my favorite time of year. Fall unofficially begins at Labor Day. That's when all of the vacationers here in Ocean City leave. The weather is still good for a month or two, but it eventually gets cooler.

I love the brisk mornings of fall. Football season starts, and hockey starts in October. There certainly are distintive colors and smells in the autumn. The leaves turn colors and it is beautiful. Fall is a time when we take our children apple and pumpkin picking. Fall is a time when we go back to school.

Fall is a time for harvest too. This the time in life where we are rewarded for our diligence in the spring and especially in the summer. If we miss that, then we miss the bounty of Fall. I love what Solomon says, that if if are not willing to plant in spring, then we will have to learn how to beg in the Fall. As we sow so we reap. It shows up in the Fall of our souls.

Fall is also a time for Halloween. It's always been a fun time for my children. None of them are Satan worshippers. They like to dress up like pirates and get their pillow cases filled with candy. Simple as that. They like to decorate pumpkins too.

Finally, Fall is a time for Thanksgiving. Is there a lovelier holiday? I don't believe so.

That's why I love the Fall.

Fall is the season of harvest:

"He will give the rain for your land in it's season, the early rain and the later rain, that you may gather your grain your wine and your oil." Deut 11:14 ESV

God sets us up for a harvest. Do you think that God does not want us to reap a harvest?

Proverbs 20:4 essentially teaches that if we do not sow in the spring, then we must learn how to beg at Harvest.

Arranging Pumpkins

Every Fall, we buy pumpkins for the kids. Each child picks out their own pumpkin. They all look the same to me, but it's amazing how they can tell which one is theirs. We always put the pumpkins in our front window, and the kids decide in what order they are to placed. Every year there is that jockeying for position on the window ledge and every morning the first order of business is … **Arranging the pumpkins.**

And heaven help the child who messes up the order of the pumpkins.

Let me assure you, I know, and they know, that there are many more important things for them to do in the morning. But for some reason those silly pumpkins became a priority in their lives.

Now, a priority is anything that takes precedence or importance over other things. For the most part we decide which things will be priorities in our lives. Naturally this is where we spend most of our time and energy.

You get a unique perspective on priority when a loved one dies, or when you read about a child that is missing. We then take a fresh look at what is most important to us. Unfortunately, those wake up calls don't usually last very long.

Jesus once warned his disciples "Where your treasure is there will your heart be also" *Matt 6:21 NIV*

We all have our pumpkins, and we spend a lot of time arranging them too. Yet God knows that there are more pressing matters at hand.

Ask yourself this "What is the one thing in my life that I know that if I gave it more attention than I do now would have incredible impact on my life and the lives of those around me?" Then ask, "If I know that to be true why am I not doing that now?"

Stop arranging the pumpkins and start rearranging your priorities.

Are You Willing to Suit Up?

Supposing the coach of the New England Patriots came up into the stands and told you **"I have the authority to give you all of the talent and ability of Tom Brady. I need you to play today. Will you suit up?"**

How many people would take that offer. I know I would. Could you imagine playing in an NFL game with the ability of a Hall of Fame quarterback? That would be exciting!

Now, that is fantasy. But actually, God makes that offer to us every day. You see, through our faith God gives us miraculous power and ability in the Holy Spirit. Unfortunately, too many folks take the gift that God offers and hide out in the bleachers as spectators.

According to the Apostle James, that is not an option. **"What good is it, my brothers, if a man claims to have faith but no deeds. Can such a faith save him?" James 2:14 (NIV)**

Christianity is more than just a change in the way you think. It's a change in the way you feel about things. It's a change in the way you behave.

This faith is not designed for spectators, but participants.

God wants you to be involved. He will give you the vision. He will give you the ability.

God is asking you today:
What kind of faith do you have?

Are you willing to suit up?

Gossip

In order for fire to be made three conditions must be met. There must be fuel to burn, and the fuel must be heated to its ignition temperature. Finally, there must be plenty of oxygen.

If you have ever seen a fire out of control, you notice that fire is not at all selective when it comes to fuel. It consumes everything in its path.

The Bible says that the tongue can be a destructive fire. You see Gossip is something that consumes everyone involved. Those of us who listen to gossip are just as guilty as those who spread it. You see, the fire won't burn if we don't provide the atmosphere for it to flourish.

The best way to control the destructive power of gossip is to extinguish it early. That could be an uncomfortable task. You may risk the friendship of the busy body. But remember, those who will gossip to you…will gossip about you.

It's all about preserving the reputation of another person and maintaining your own dignity.

When you defend those who are absent, you almost always retain the trust of those who are present.

Check Your Motives

Apparently God has become the perpetrator of some
grand pyramid scam. The purpose of this scheme
is to shower prosperity on the chosen few who
have somehow figured out the secret formula.

Here's how the plan works. You send your money to
God's anointed spokesman, and because of your faithful
giving, God will grant you abounding prosperity.

The only glitch that I can see is that not everyone is
prospering. The anointed spokesmen are becoming
very wealthy, but God seems to be welshing on
the faithful giver. Maybe they have to give more
or maybe they have to pray more intensely.

A. W. Tozer wrote, **"The spiritual quality of a prayer
is determined not by intensity, but by its origin."**

Does an obsession for material possessions and worldly
success really originate in the Holy Spirit?

Does a new car, a bigger house, or an
expensive suit really glorify God?

Does the world really need one more self-indulgent Christian?

Now the Apostle James says that disappointment comes because we ask with the wrong motives. Our intentions are to spend what we get on our fleshly pleasures.

I think it's high time that the American church starts showing some spiritual maturity – stop marching to the world's parade.

**We need to look at what motivates us
and determine the origin.**

The Real Heroes

Fall is the time of the year for the World Series.
That's when we crown Baseball's best team for the
year. And the winner always gets a parade.

Nobody does parades better than NYC. I remember, one
year they held a parade for the Yankees when they won the
World Series, and a million and a half people came. It was
spectacular. Shortly after that week they held the Veteran's
Day parade, but only a few thousand showed up for that.

Somehow we have skewed our sense of priorities.

Don't we owe a debt of gratitude to these veterans?

**The church has it's own veterans too, but we
really don't honor their memory either.**

These are the saints who were obedient to God
and paved the way for us even though they never
realized the promises they were proclaiming.

Peter writes:
**"It was revealed to them that they were not serving
themselves but you, when they spoke of the things
that have now been told to you by those who have
preached the Gospel......"** 1 Peter 1:12 (NIV)

Don't we owe these folks a debt of gratitude?

I'll bet that most of us know more about Babe
Ruth and Lou Gehrig than we know about the
prophets or the early church fathers.

Who are our real heroes anyway?

A Fine Example

I had a friend who was reprimanded for reading the Bible and preaching at work. She insisted that she was being persecuted. But she wasn't being persecuted she was being a jerk.

Our greatest message to anyone is by being an excellent example.

A cheerful industrious employee is a better witness than any preaching.

Peter said:
"...that by doing right you may silence the ignorance of foolish men" 1Peter 2:15 (NIV)

We make the biggest impact by the way we live our lives.

By doing right Peter expects that we **"honor all men"**

"submit ourselves to those in authority"

And when we are treated unjustly
"...endure it with patience"

I don't know about you but that goes against the grain of my pride. You see, I'm more apt to stand up for my rights than I am to; **endure with patience.**

These are the hallmarks of Christian discipleship though.

And you can choose for people to look at your life and say, **"There goes a fine example"** or **"There goes a jerk!"**

Showing Thanks

My mom used to say, "If you can't be thankful for the things you have, at least be thankful for the things you don't have." That's sound advice!

You see, Thanksgiving is more than football games and parades. It's more than a big turkey dinner. It's a state of mind!

Maybe we should ask ourselves
Are we thankful?

And what should that thankfulness produce in us?
Do we just say "Thanks God", and move on?

Shouldn't our appreciation for God's blessings move us to a more devoted life?

Look, God knows our hearts, but maybe
He expects a more visible sign of our appreciation.

We certainly honor God when our thankful hearts produce acts of mercy and generosity to others. Actually, Jesus identifies so closely to these acts of kindness that He tells us that whenever we perform acts of charity for even the least of His brothers:

<u>We do it for Him</u>

So maybe Thanksgiving is not so much looking inward for feelings of appreciation, but looking outward for opportunities to express it.

Wake-up Call

A psychologist surveyed 3000 people and asked them,
"What do you have to live for?" More than 90% were
simply enduring the present looking forward to some
future event. Waiting to retire. Waiting for their children
to grow up…or even waiting for someone else to die.

Isn't that sad that most people have no passion
for the present, or vision for today? They spend
so much time looking for something better in the
future that they miss God's mission now.

But that's not an option!

You see, Jesus told us to occupy until He returns. He
said to be on guard, be busy, don't be caught sleeping.

Judging from that survey though, most
people are sleepwalking.

Well, here is the wake-up call!!!

God has something special for your
life, but the work starts today.

I guess what most people don't realize is that the future is
by and large determined by the way we live the present!

What does God have special for your life?

What is God calling you to?

Is There Vacancy in Your Heart?

It was the responsibility of a herald to prepare the way for a coming King. He would make sure that the roads were safe, and clear. And he would alert every one of the King's arrival.

It must have been a position of honor and prestige. I could see where someone might get carried away with their own importance, but truly, they were only there to make way for the King.

John the Baptist was the Herald for Jesus. He was there to prepare the hearts of men. Although Jesus doesn't come with the same pomp and hullabaloo as any other dignitary, His arrival is a magnificent event. It was the intersection of eternity with time.

It is that coming King that we celebrate each year at Advent. Amidst all of the hustle and bustle of the holiday season we miss the point that this is more than a one-time event in history. His birth may have been 2000 years ago, but His presence is no less real today.

Today the Holy Spirit prepares men's hearts to make way for the coming of the King. Not for a visit the arrangements are more permanent now.

You see, God's not interested in visiting your heart and then moving on – He's interested in moving in.

Is there vacancy in your heart?

Church History

When I went to Ireland, I learned a lot about Irish history, and saw some beautiful Landscape. Standing in a monastery built nearly 1600 years ago, by young men half my age I gained a new perspective on Christian History.

It gave me a sense that I was part of something a lot bigger than I ever realized.

Unfortunately, most of us don't know a lot about the saints who sacrificed everything to preserve the faith. We probably know more about Rock and Roll history than we do Church history.

Isn't that a tragic reality?

Dr. Thomas Gibbs wrote:
"Every man has leaned upon the past. Every liberty we enjoy has been bought at an incredible cost. There is not a privilege, nor an opportunity that is not the product of other men's labors. We drink every day from wells we have not dug. We warm ourselves by fires we have not kindled...no man lives unto himself alone. All the past is invested in him. A new day is a good time to say, 'I am under the obligation to accept my share of the world's grief, my share of its opportunities."

We give our children a lot of things, but if we don't give them a knowledge of their heritage in the faith we have failed.

Are we sharing in our share of the world's grief or the world's opportunities?

We owe it to those who have gone before us.

Was Hosea a Chump?

Hosea was a prophet in the Old Testament. His wife, Gomer, was, shall we say, less than faithful. The kind of woman that most men would be glad to lose. But Hosea didn't feel that way. Time and time again she would run off with someone, and time and time again he would welcome her back.

Finally, when she has reached the depths of her depravity, Hosea pays to redeem her. He is the one who has been betrayed. He is the one who has been wronged. And yet he pays the price. *Hos 3 NIV*

Can you understand this guy?

He is either the biggest sap in history-

OR

the most loving, graceful husband who ever lived.

Actually the life of Hosea is a lesson about the longsuffering love of God. What God is showing is that we can't exhaust his forgiveness. No matter how low we sink, His love is beyond our comprehension. In God's eyes there are no hopeless causes.

Now would God go as far as Hosea?

**Would He personally come and pay
the price for our redemption?**

**If He would, then to reject that love; to reject that
forgiveness, would be the ultimate act of foolishness.**

Wouldn't it?

Where is Your Kingdom?

In Luke chapter 23, Pontius Pilate asked
Jesus, "Are you the King of the Jews?"

Now, how could this guy be a king?
Born in a stable
His father was a carpenter…his mother a peasant
He had no palace
He had no army
He had no authority (or so it seemed)

"My kingdom is not of this world" He explained.
And those who would pledge allegiance to Him would
have to look beyond palaces; beyond the usual pomp
and circumstance that goes with earthly royalty.

"The kingdom of God is within you"
(*Luke 17:21 KJ21*) He explained.

To Which Kingdom do you pledge your allegiance?
That's easy to tell isn't it? Just look around
You…just look in your heart.

Would you like something bigger than this world offers?
Would you like to experience something
deeper this holiday season?

Certain traditions call this the Advent season.
It is a celebration of the coming of Jesus.
The Advent of His birth
The Advent of Truth

"Those committed to truth will hear my voice" He testified

Are you committed to the truth?

The truth about you?
The truth about Him?

It All Starts with Prayer

My neighbor's son died suddenly. It was
a dark time for the family, and our whole
neighborhood. My children knew him well.

I bought some pizzas for the family. My son Jonathan
came with me. We delivered the pizza to the family
and left. Jonathan wanted to know if we were going
to stay and eat the pizza with them. "No," I said,"…
we just want to make sure they have dinner."

Years later after Super Storm Sandy, Jonathan and I delivered
Thanksgiving Dinner to people in our town who had been
flooded out. Jonathan was getting a taste of works of charity.

In Jesus' teaching, it is not simply works of
charity and deeds of mercy, which He insists
upon, but inward spiritual character.

The Christian faith calls us to a purity of life that is
far beyond our capacity. And yet despite that, we still
feel the pull and the yearning to be sanctified.

Prayer offers a solution that is infinitely superior to our
own manipulations, or formulas. Prayer establishes an
inward character, which influences our conduct.

Weakness of character betrays a feeble prayer life.

Jack Hayford says, "Hell reigns where heaven is not invited."

Great people of God are great people of prayer.
Hell is not reigning in their lives.

What a tragedy to have a life lived that makes
no impact for the Kingdom of God.

I am determined not to let that happen in my life.

E. M. Bounds, a civil war chaplan, wrote:
"Praying which does not result in changed
character, and Holy conduct is a farce."
That's pretty strong, but it rings true to
me, and I am up to the challenge.

Playground or Battleground

After Thanksgiving comes the time of year
when we celebrate the Birth of Christ.

It's a great time; I love this season!

But amidst all of the festivities let us never lose sight
of the magnitude of His coming. The implications
are as real today as they were 2000 years ago.

He told us **"Do not suppose that I have come to
bring peace to the earth. I did not come to bring
peace, but a sword." Matthew 10:34 (NIV)**

These are words that would suggest that we are
involved in some sort of altercation. It is the struggle
between a redeemed and an unredeemed world.

A.W. Tozer once wrote, "...*tremendous spiritual forces are
present in the world. Humanity, because of its spiritual nature,
is caught in the middle. Evil powers are bent on destroying
us, while Christ is present to save us through the power of
the Gospel*" The World: Playground or Battleground?

The problem, he sites is that today, people think of the
world not as a battleground, but as a playground. **"We are
not here to fight"** he laments, **"We are here to frolic"**

But Jesus warns us **"Be on guard. Lest your spirits
become bloated with indulgences, and drunkenness,
and worldly cares." Luke 21:34 (NET)**

This is the time of Year when we celebrate
the "Birth of Christ" It's a lot of fun!

Maybe this year you can take a step back
from the festivities and ask yourself:

"Does there need to be a new birth
of His urgency in my life?"

Just another Christmas?

This is a busy time of year!

Most people have a lot of work to do to
prepare for the coming of Christmas.

There's cooking to be done, decorating, and of course,
loads of shopping. When you really get involved
with Christmas it's pretty exciting. But there's a bit
of a let down when it's over. We go back to a regular
way of life with the same hum-drum attitude.

But, with a change of heart Christmas can be
more than a passing holiday this year.

In preparing for the coming of Jesus, John
the Baptist spoke to the hearts of men.

Through repentance of sin this would be more than a
celebrity appearance. Christ's arrival would have an
enduring effect on hearts and lives would change direction.

Today, the Holy Spirit works as the front man for Jesus.
He's looking to exchange our old attitudes and prejudices
with the Love of Christ. A more enduring Holiday Spirit.

This year with a change of heart, you can make
Christmas more than a passing holiday.

Can you focus on making this Christmas
more than a passing holiday?

107

What More Shall we Do?

After hearing John the Baptist preach, many people were moved to be baptized. But they sensed that baptism and repentance were not the destination, but simply the first step. With anticipation, they asked him…What more shall we do?

To the common people he said give. If you have 2 coats give one away. If you have extra food you should share. **How many of us have so much more than we need?**

To the tax collectors he says don't take more than is required. Be honest. Be reasonable. **Isn't every business transaction a test of our character?**

To the soldiers he says don't abuse your authority and be content with your pay.

How often do we miss an opportunity to exercise character in authority? And instead of leading with conscience, we let our egos take over.

John was showing us that our faith is more than a public show of our wish to change, but a daily commitment to demonstrate that change.

Beyond our baptism
Beyond our weekly affirmation of our faith

How many of us possess the courage to ask

"What more shall we do?"

Too Late!

I had a German professor who had one rule for class.
"Wenn Sie spat Kommen, Kommen Sie zu spat"

Loosely translated "If you come late…you're too late!"
I can't tell you how many kids came late only to find
the door locked. And pitifully, they would stand there
looking in the window, but they weren't getting in.
They were too late!

She meant what she said:
Be on time and be prepared!!

How many opportunities do you think we miss
because we are late or unprepared?

In the parable of the Ten Virgins, Jesus warns of
the perils of being too late or unprepared.

Waiting for the bridegroom, five of them realize that their
lamps are out of oil. They didn't bring enough to last the night.
They were unprepared.

Then, while they are out searching for more oil, the
bridegroom returns. He takes the five that are prepared
Him, and by the time the others return they're shut out.
They came too late!

"Be on the alert", Jesus says **"for you do
not know the day nor the hour."**

A lot of us are holding lamps out there. It looks good to everyone else, but only we know if there is enough fuel to last. I have to assume that like that German professor, Jesus meant what He said.

Don't be caught unprepared.
Take some time out and check the Oil.

John 3:16

You know, you can't always trust people who quote the Bible. That may sound strange, but some of the most inscrutable people have used the Bible to justify their nefarious deeds.

I suppose, if you had cause, you could pretty much get the Bible to say anything you wanted. Even the Devil quoted the Bible. He was trying to divert Jesus from His task, and tempting Him to make a frivolous display of His power. Now everyone knows Satan as the epitome of evil, but he quoted the Bible.

Jesus knows the Bible too, and He answers the temptation **"You are not to put the Lord your God to the test."** Luke 4:12 (ESV)

You see, it is possible to have a head filled with Scripture and a heart in opposition to God. I see it all the time.

Be careful though. Don't be swayed by the words themselves, but be transformed by the truths they portray.

And the truth is that God's most awesome show of power and faithfulness was displayed on the Cross.

And the Cross demonstrates how much God Loves us.

And the message of Christmas is summed up in John 3:16 **"For God so loved the world that He gave His only son, so that all who believe in Him will not perish, but have eternal life."** (NIV)

Clean Sweep

The New York Times once fired some employees for distributing offensive e-mails at work. The Times didn't appreciate that its computers were being used to pass around vulgar jokes.

What surprised many of the employees was that they thought that the messages had been deleted. Actually, they were deleted, but were not completely gone. Somewhere in the archives of the computer system were all of the e-mails, and the company was able to retrieve them.

They were able to delete the information on the surface, but it took a higher authority to clear out the archives.

Think about that for a minute.

How many times have you resisted forgiving someone? On the surface you think that you have, but somewhere in the archives of your memory you still hold a grudge.

Jesus Said:

"If you forgive men for their transgressions your heavenly father will also forgive you. But if you don't forgive men, then your father will not forgive your transgressions." Matt 6:14 (NASB)

That sounds pretty serious doesn't it?

I wouldn't want to be held accountable for
what is archived in my memory.

It's time for a clean sweep.

But it takes a supernatural grace to do that.

It takes the Grace of God to truly forgive.

The Nature of Worship

A man stricken with leprosy came to Jesus, and
on his knees, asks **"Lord, if you are willing,
you can make me clean."** Matt 8:2 (NIV)

Jesus, moved by compassion, heals the man.

It was the humble spirit of the man that impresses me. He
didn't come demanding a healing. He didn't come claiming a
healing. He simply said, **"Lord if you are willing, you can…"**

I was telling my friend that, unlike this man, we
seemed to have lost our respect for God.

"It's not out of respect that we come to God", she
said, "We **approach Him with adoration"**

That's the key isn't it?

We respect our parents. We respect our friends,
and those in authority, but the very nature of God
demands that we come with something deeper.

It says that the man came **"worshipping Jesus."**

True worship requires that we empty ourselves,
and come to God **"with a delightful sense of
admiring awe and astonished wonder."**

It is our idea of God that determines the depth of our worship, and the depth of our worship that determines the miracles that we experience.

He didn't come with great fanfare. There was no extravagant production. He was a humble leper with a simple prayer, but he received a remarkable healing.

Winter

When I was growing up, winter didn't bother me all that much. It was cold, but we didn't notice it. There was a drainage sump at the end of my street and it had some pretty good hills. The whole neighborhood use to ride their sleds there in the winter. It was owned by the township and it was fenced in with a lock on the gate. That was not a problem for us. My dog Buster, always came with us to enjoy the snow.

After riding our sleds for hours we would go home and my mother would make us hot chocolate and toll-house squares. We didn't seem to mind the winter. It bothers me now.

You have to persevere to survive the winter.
Some places winter is really cold:

"From it's chamber comes the whirlwind, and cold from the scattering winds. By the breath of God ice is given, and the broad waters are frozen fast." Job 37:9 (NIV)

Some winters are a lot more severe than others, Its not all sleigh riding and hot chocolate. It can be like, what Saint John of the Cross described as the Dark Night of the Soul, and we all have those dark cold nights. It can be an illness, a divorce, or a death of a loved one. No one is immune to a personal winter. It can be beautiful outside, and dark and cold in our souls. Sometimes the winter is so dark, it is so cold, it is so depressing, that we just need to see a little green.

I heard Jim Rohn once explain that the work of winter is to draw upon the productivity of every other season. The winter is when we draw upon the spiritual disciplines that we have practiced all year. We can never let the bleakness of winter lead us to decide…"Everything is over", because its not. The winter will soon be the past and then…Spring. And Spring comes every year.

"Your life does not get better by chance, it gets better by change." Jim Rohn

If we can change the way we react to the winters of life, by preparing every other season, then our lives will change dramatically.

The Womb and the Compassion of God

❄✳

Linguistics is the study of the structure, function and acquisition of language. One of the more interesting areas of study is historical linguistics and the derivation of words. Where they come from and how they come to mean what they mean today.

Anyone who studies the Bible should pay particular attention to the original meanings of the words used in the text. You don't have to know ancient Greek or Hebrew to do this. You can rely on the most respected scholars in history.

Years ago I read that the Hebrew words frequently used for the **Compassion of God and the Womb of a Woman** are derived from the same root word, "racha-".

This is an interesting correlation isn't it?

What is it about a mother's womb that so resembles the Compassion of God?

The womb of a mother totally envelops the child.

The womb is the child's only source of nourishment and protection.

The womb is the place of a new creation.

Even more fascinating that these two Hebrew words would be so closely related is the fact that the greatest show of God's Compassion came through the Womb of a Woman.

"For God so loved the world that He gave His one and only Son, that whosoever believes in Him Shall not perish but have eternal Life. For God did not send His Son to condemn the world, but to save the world" John 3:16

We could use a dose of that enveloping love this year, couldn't we?

I want to wish you a Merry Christmas, but also a new birth of God's compassion in your heart this year.

The Great Paradox

❄

Eight days after the birth of Jesus, His parents
Mary and Joseph take Him to the temple for His
circumcision. It's there where they meet up with
Simeon, a man, who the Bible says was **"righteous and
devout, full of the Holy Spirit." Luke 2:25 (NIV)**

When he sees Jesus he immediately recognizes that this child
is the promise of God, the Messiah. He takes the baby in his
arms and sings the praises of God for His salvation. "Now
that I have held you in my arms," he says, "my life can come to
an end." He has seen the fruit of God's promise of deliverance.

And when he gives the baby back he says the most curious
thing to Mary. He tells her that because of this child
**"…a sword will pierce even your own soul."
Luke 2 25:35 (NIV)**

It's interesting, isn't it? That the deepest things we learn from
God are more often the result of suffering and not prosperity.

But this is the great paradox…isn't it? The King
of Kings…God's chosen One, The Messiah; is born
in a manger amongst farm animals and will die on
a cross between two thieves. A most unlikely hero.
That is not the way that I would have written it.

And this is what makes believing in Him such a mystery.

Now depending how you look at it, it is a
life of tragedy or a life of triumph.

*Simeon, a man who depended on the promises of God, and was
filled with the Holy Spirit saw The Life of Christ as a triumph.*

121

A Pear Grows on a Cherry Tree

❋✻

There are nearly 70,000 species of trees on the earth. Botanists identify them by their bark and foliage. I figure the best way to tell them apart is to see what is growing on them.

If I see an apple growing I know that it's an apple tree, even if it looks like a pear tree and has a pear tree sign on it if it is growing apples it is an apple tree. My Dad bought four trees to plant in our backyard. He thought that he bought four cherry trees. One for each of us kids.

One of the trees grew pears. It was a pear tree. But my Dad insisted that he bought four cherry trees. My mother would egg him on, "Andy your cherry tree is growing pears again. Just to spite you." He would never admit that he bought a pear tree by mistake. Maybe there was a tag that said Cherry, but it was a pear tree.

People are the same way too. Oh, they claim to be a lot of things, but I want to see the fruit.

John the Baptist told his early followers **"Bring forth fruit of your repentance"**, and then he says, **"The ax is already at the root of the trees, and every tree that does not produce good fruits will be cut down and thrown into the fire."** Matt 3:8 (NIV)

Theologians have argued over what he meant by that. I'm no theologian, but it sure sounds like a pretty clear warning to me. **Good trees bear good fruit.**

But more than that; Good trees have solid roots. Roots that go deep and nourish the tree, but also steady it in when the storms come. Good trees give something of themselves too. You see most trees possess the ability to produce more trees...Maybe even a forest.

What about YOU?

Are you a tree with strong roots bearing good fruit or are you just a sap?

Change...Real Change

For many of us the New Year is an opportunity for a new beginning. We don't just change our calendar, we psyche ourselves up with resolutions that next year we are going to improve.

We're going to stop smoking and start exercising. We're going to lose weight and make more money. Next year is going to be better. Next Year is going to be better.

The good news is that we recognize that there is room for improvement in our lives. That's a good beginning. Unfortunately, by the second week in January, our resolutions have gone by the wayside. We're disappointed and we're discouraged.

But recognizing the need for change, and desiring to be changed are no substitute for developing the RESOLVE to make those changes.

You see, change, real change, happens from the inside out. "I'll give you a new heart", **God says** "You're gonna see things differently, and you're gonna have a new perspective. You're gonna be a new creation." Ezekiel 36:26 (paraphrasee)

I'll tell you what – I'm gonna take Him up on that.

I'm going to listen more.

**I'm not going to look to be blessed as much
as I am going to look to be a blessing.**

And next year...

Next year is going to be better.

Good Habits...Good Roots

❄

My friend John is an impressive guy. I have always
admired his discipline. As long as I know him he
has exercised regularly and watched his diet. He
has a positive outlook on life and a strong faith.

You'd think that would be enough to guarantee good health,
but John developed cancer. A very aggressive brain cancer.

I see an irony here – maybe even cruel injustice. But John
doesn't see it that way. In fact, he says that if it weren't
for all that exercise, his good attitude and strong faith the
cancer would have killed him. He wasn't thinking about
cancer all those years he was just developing good habits.

**And good habits are like strong roots -
They always bear fruit.**

The book of Psalms says, "The one who delights in the
law of the Lord will be a firmly rooted tree bearing
good fruit in season." Psalm 1:3 paraphrase

In the seasons to come you are going to face
crises. There is no doubt about that!

Maybe you should consider where you spend your time now.

**Because the roots you develop today will determine
whether you wither under pressure or flourish with Fruit.**

Proverbs 18:16

❀✲

Wayne Dyer said that we should not die with our song still in our soul.

You see, God has deposited in each of us a measure
of talents and abilities. And those gifts, the Bible says,
shall make room for you. Room to demonstrate them in
your family, in your church, and in your community.

When you are willing to share your
gifts...there is room for you.

Now, some day God is going to conduct an
audit of the deposit He has made.

Where will you stand in that audit?

Have you squandered your talents?

Never using them at all?

In that case, you can expect no reward.

Have you hoarded your talents?
Using them for your own fame and glory?
In that case, you have received your reward in full.

Or have you invested your gift in God's Kingdom?
In that case you will not only receive a reward
now but also a reward that will last forever.

God has an excellent plan for reinvestment.

One that pays dividends for all eternity.

One that makes room for us.

A Great Head of Hair

❄✳

Absalom was an interesting guy. He was the
son of King David. He had everything going
for him, especially a great head of hair.

Every year he would parade into town and get his annual
haircut. Then he would weigh it. That is a strange habit, but
this guy really dug his hair. 2 Samuel 14:25-26 (paraphrase)

Unfortunately the thing that gave him the greatest
sense of pride eventually led to his downfall. During his
rebellion against his father's kingdom, Absalom found
himself running for his life. He ran into a tree and his
hair got caught in the branches, and there he hung, and
there he was slain. 2 Samuel 18:9,14 (paraphrase)

But it wasn't the length of his hair that did
him in, it was the hardness of his heart.

If David gave Absalom more power
would he have been happy?

If David made Absalom King would he have been Happy?

Jesus asked his disciples "For what would it profit a man if
he gains the whole world, and forfeits his soul? Or what will
a man give in exchange for his soul?" Matt 16:26 (ASB)

- **What would it take to make you happy?**
- **Do you want power, prestige, or money?**
- **Or how about a great head of hair?**

What would you give in exchange for your soul?

Jesus is There

One Sunday while he was on vacation, President Bush, the elder, was visiting a church in Maine. Word got around that he would be there, but because of security reasons no one could know which service he would attend.

A woman asked the Pastor, "Could you tell me which service the President will attend"

"For reasons of security, I can't tell you that", answered the Pastor," But you should know that Jesus Christ will be at both services."

You see, Jesus promised His disciples that whenever two or three are gathered in His name He would be among them.(Matt 18:20) Every time we go to church and gather in Jesus' name…He is there.

People tell me that they don't go to church for a lot of reasons. They don't like the music, or they don't like the preaching. Some say that they just find church boring.

The primary reason for going to church is not so that you will be entertained. It's not about you. It's because He is there.

I know some people don't go to church because there are too many hypocrites there.

But as Zig Ziglar once said, "You just come any way, there is always room for one more."

Radio Prizes

❄

During the golden years of radio many of
the most popular shows offered these great
premiums. Souvenirs that you could buy.
There was the Buck Rogers Ring of Saturn,
Space Patrol's Project –O-Scope, and of course
Jack Armstrong's Egyptian Code Whistle.

The Egyptian Code whistle came with a code book to teach
you how to whistle in code and how to interpret it. Anyone
could hear the whistle, but only the initiated could understand.

St. Thomas Acquinas explained spiritual things in sort of the
same way. He wasn't selling decoder books, but what he said
was that unless we are enlightened by the Holy Spirit: We may
read the Gospel and we may hear the Gospel, but something
is missing. What is missing is a touch of the Holy Spirit.

Traveling to the Sea of Galilee, Jesus came across a deaf
man. He had come to Jesus to be healed. Without any
fanfare, without any hoopla, Jesus took him aside and
touched him with a healing touch. The man began to hear
clearly and speak plainly. Mark 7:31-37 (paraphrase)

**Maybe that's what we all need from time to
time...a little aside with Him... a touch to
open our eyes...our ears... our hearts.**

Not just to understand what is going on in church, but to see what God is doing in our lives and the lives of those around us.

**We need to encounter the secret decoder
of God's infinite wisdom:**

That touch of HIS Spirit!

The Whole Truth

❄✳
❄

Do you ever feel like you never really get the whole truth?

Whether you're buying something, listening to a politician, looking at a new job…Nobody ever gives the whole story.

My son Jason is always questioning, "Are we getting the whole story?"

But, it could be that people don't want the whole story. When Paul Tsongas was running for President he said, that the American people don't really want to elect a President, they want to elect Santa Claus. I guess he was saying that American voters don't want to hear the truth, they want to hear empty promises.

Then we are up in arms when the politicians can't deliver.

Maybe I'm different, but I prefer to know what I should expect and what's going to be expected of me. I can live with the negatives.

I say I can live with the negatives…as long as the positives outweigh them.

Somehow people have gotten the impression that as long as they make some vague profession of faith, the balance of their lives doesn't reflect any change. No matter how they live their lives they will always be Christians. Is that the whole truth?

I don't think so. But, I'm not a theologian.

Jesus was never very vague or misleading
about what He expected.

"If anyone wishes to come after me, let him deny himself,
take up his cross and follow me. Whoever saves his life
will lose it. But whoever loses his life for my sake or the
sake of the Gospel will find it" Matt 16:24-25 NASB

That's full and fair disclosure isn't it?
Is that an accurate description of your faith?
Maybe you've bought into a cross-less Christianity.

To tell you plainly...That's not the whole truth!

Living Against the Grain

❄❄

Our participation in God's grace, the extent of our effectiveness in His kingdom has nothing to do with what we are willing to give _to_ God and everything to do with what we are willing to give _up for_ God.

The 12 Apostles were bickering amongst themselves as to who would be the greatest of Jesus' disciples. They had ambitions toward heavenly things but with fleshly intentions.

- What did they think would be the status of Christ's greatest disciple?
- Did they think that they would they be recognized wherever they went?
- Would other men envy them?
- Would they be rich?
- What would be the status of Christ's greatest disciple?

Jesus told them that if you wish to be first you must be last of all, and servant of all. If you want to be great in God's eyes you must be willing to be lowly in the eyes of men. Matt 20:27

That runs contrary to the very core of our hearts. Everything within us says…

- Look at me
- Notice me
- Appreciate me

The call of Christ is a call for a radical change in
our character, our will, and our conduct.

What a magnificent paradox:

If you want to be first you must be willing
to be last, and servant of all.

Escape Velocity

❄❅

In astronautics we learn that more power and
energy is expended during lift off and in clearing
the earth's gravity than in navigating a million
miles and returning again to earth.

**The energy needed to escape the earth's
atmosphere is called "Escape Velocity."**

**Actually, the point is that our past, our trauma, and
our wounds exert such a powerful pull on our lives,
that only courageous energy and effort will free us.**

I think that is what Jesus is showing us when He said,

"If your hand is your downfall, cut it off! Better for
you to enter life maimed than to go to hell with both
hands. If your leg is your downfall, cut it off! Better for
you to enter into life crippled, than go to hell with both
feet. And if you're your eye is your downfall, tear it out!
Better for you to enter God's Kingdom with one eye than
to go to Hell with both eyes." Matt 9:43-47 NASB

**He's not talking about self-mutilation. What He is saying
is that our fallen nature has wielded such power for so long
that only a violent extraction from our soul will free us.**

**Now, some people might view a need for change
as a sign of weakness and failure, but really
it is a sign of courage and commitment.**

What is it in your life that is your downfall?
Are you ready for that courageous break?

To tell you the truth, for such a deep seeded
change, it's going to take more than just courage.
More than just "Escape Velocity."

It's going to take supernatural Grace!

Life Centered in God

❄❄

A man came to Jesus and asked him;
Which is the first of all commandments?

What is the one thing, above everything
else, that typifies what God wants?

Jesus answered:
The Lord our God is Lord alone. Therefore
you shall love the Lord your God:

- With all your heart
- With all your soul
- With all your mind
- And with all your strength

In other words:

All that our heart desires — the things that we spend
our lives pursuing, should be substituted for a love for
God. Set your affections on things above. Paul said
that all of our soul, the very essence of who we are, our
personality, our ID, should be anchored in Him.

All of our mind. Take every thought captive, the
Apostle tells us, and put it into subjection to Him.

And finally, love Him with all of our strength. There is
something magnificent about the human spirit. A well of
strength, which we draw from in our most desperate times.
Jesus says let those wells be filled with living waters.

The life centered in God examines:

- What it is that captivates our hearts?
  - Occupies our minds?
  - And drains our strength?

Certainly, this is a life most of us overlook.

And we overlook it in favor of what?

Dividing the Holy Land

❄❊

When the Lord was dividing the Holy Land between the Israelites, He made no provision for the tribe of Levi. They would not own nor possess any of the Promise Land. The Levites were the Priestly tribe, and God told them;

"I am your portion and your inheritance among
the sons of Israel." Numbers 18:20 (ASB)

Their lives would be completely given over to religious service. Their inheritance, and their security, was not tied to this world. They would be heirs to an Heavenly estate.

God had miraculously delivered them
for something great in Him.

My son Joseph was born three months premature.
His life was so fragile. He was less than three pounds.
He was the beneficiary of many prayers, and he
lived and has thrived, and now he is a man.

I have always thought that God had something
special planned for Joseph. A touch on his heart.
A purpose for that remarkable recovery.

Those of us who are believers in Christ have been
told that we are members of a royal Priesthood. We
have as our high priest, someone far superior to any
Levite, and our part, our inheritance is in HIM.

No amount of money, no political candidate, nothing that this world has to offer, will measure up to His surpassing Glory. We need to develop minds and hearts that are other-worldly.

Remember: Our security, Our future,
our inheritance is in Him.

Forty Days of Change

❄❄

This is the time of year when we begin the season most of us know as Lent. Lent is a 40-day period before Easter. The intention of this season is to practice sacrifice and self-denial. Not because we want other people to see how religious we can be, or that we think we can impress God, but we want to, in some way, demonstrate how profoundly we are touched by His sacrifice.

Now, the observance of Lent has always been associated with the more traditional churches in Christianity. But in the past 10 years or so, more and more Evangelical denominations have adopted it. Look, it's a great idea.

It's a time of fasting and prayer, an opportunity for self-examination; to reflect on the crucifixion, and give thanks for the Resurrection.

E. M. Bounds once wrote:

"It is not the intellectually great that the Church needs; nor is it men of wealth that the times demand. It is not people of great social influence that this day requires. Above everybody and everything else, it is people of faith, people of mighty prayer, men and women after the fashion of the saints and heroes enumerated in Hebrews, who obtained "a good report through faith", that the church and the whole wide world of humanity needs." – The Complete Works of E.M. Bounds

I'd like to challenge you this year to take these 40 days of Lent and submit yourself to fasting and prayer. Choose someone or something in your life to pray for and go for it.

It will change your heart and it will reap great blessings.

I know that it will!

I Thirst

I Thirst
Jesus reminds us of His humanity, when he cries
out from the Cross, "I thirst" John 19:28 NIV.
"I thirst", sounds like a uniquely human declaration…
I thirst!
But in this brief statement, Jesus identifies
with all of creation…doesn't he?
Because ALL of creation thirsts…

Humans thirst…Animals thirst…Plants thirst.
Even the parched dry ground thirsts.
All of Creation Thirsts!

I can tell you that I have a lot thirsts.
I thirst for success…I thirst for recognition…
I thirst for Safety, Security and Happiness.

What do you thirst for?
Do you thirst to be appreciated?
To be loved?
To be heard or understood?
Or do you thirst…just to be seen?
These aren't bad things, but they will never
quench the deeper thirst in our Soul.
The Psalmist tells us of that thirst:
*"As the Deer pants for streams water, so my soul
pants for you oh God." Psalm 42:1 NIV*

Have you ever seen desperate thirst?
Years ago, radio host, Paul Harvey told a story
about the drought in the Australian Outback.
The deer were dying of thirst and they would come out
to the railroad tracks in the morning to sip the dew.
They were so thirsty, that when the trains came they
could not turn away and some would be killed.
That is a desperate thirst!

I need to develop that desperate thirst for God. A thirst
so desperate, that when the world threatens to run me
down...my parched heart cannot turn from Him.
Jesus promised that whoever drinks of the water that
He offers will never thirst again... John 4:13 NIV.
In fact, He promised that out of our inner beings
would flow Rivers of Living Water, Refreshing
all of those around us. John 7:38 NIV.
I want that!

St. Augustine wrote, *"You have made us for yourself, O
Lord, and our heart is restless until it rests in you."*

How restless are our hearts today?

Take a moment and close your eyes...be silent for
20 seconds...and whisper "Lord I thirst"
See how God refreshes us!

Check Your Resume

One of my favorite passages from the Bible comes from the Apostle Paul's letter to the church in Phillipi. In one section of the letter he writes:

"That I might know Him and the power of His resurrection, and the fellowship of His suffering, being conformed unto His death." Phil 3:10 NASB

I have always thought that this is an amazingly powerful statement, but I am amazed how often it is only partially quoted. You see a lot of folks like the first part of Paul's quote. Who wouldn't want to know God on a deeper level and experience His resurrection power? Come on…

But who wants to get behind the fellowship of His suffering, or being conformed unto His death? That doesn't sound like fun!

And what kind of suffering is Paul talking about here? Is it mental suffering or actual physical suffering? Isn't God about joy, peace, and fun?

Jesus said that the world would hate his followers because it first hated him. Would you be willing to sacrifice your reputation and suffer the humiliation of ridicule for Him?

And what about being conformed unto His death? Paul also said that we are always carrying about in our body's the dying of Christ.

How many of us would sign on for that?

Paul used as his credentials the fact that he had given up everything for Christ – position, power, and reputation. He was beaten near death several times, he was shipwrecked, destitute, and abandoned. But that was his resume and the resume of Christians all over the world today. How about you?

Have you checked your resume lately?

Crossing the Jordan

The children of Israel had wandered the wilderness
for 40 years. Standing before the Promised Land only
one obstacle stood before them; The Jordan River.
And at this time of the year the river was at a flood
level, and yet God told them that within three days
they would cross the river on foot. Joshua 1 NASB

It was an unthinkable proposition, but
a glorious illustration for us.

God instructed Joshua to have the priests carry the Ark of
the Covenant, the symbol of God's presence in their midst,
down to the water, and step in. Then when the water parts
all the people shall cross over with their eyes on the Ark.

The water did part and they crossed over.
All the way on dry land.

How many times do we get a glimpse of God's promises
in our lives, but a river of problems keeps us from it. I'm
not talking about problems like; Oh, I wish I was more
prosperous or my bills are too high. I'm talking about
high water marks of devastation. Things like people
dying and families falling apart. These are the kinds of
problems that flood our lives and muddy our souls.

We stand on the banks, and say "There is
just no way of getting through this."

But God says, even to us today, that we need to put Him middle of the problem, and keep our eyes on Him. Over and over again the Lord tells Joshua "Be Strong and Courageous" *Joshua 1:9 NASB*

That's what we need today.

Keep our eyes on Him and we will pass through it on dry land. Our feet will not be muddied.

Change Someone Else's Life

Every year at Lent I devote that time to fasting and prayer. Not because I am some holy guy, but I believe that it is a powerful practice. Going in, I don't know what I am going to pray about, but someone or some situation always come to mind, and I focus on those.

Several years ago right around that time I heard that someone once close to me was in prison. That broke my heart. I hadn't spoken to him in over ten years and I had no way of getting in touch with him, but I decided to pray for him.

I prayed that God would touch his life, and that in some miraculous way I could get in touch with him. This week, out of nowhere, I received a letter from him from jail. I don't know how he got my address, but he wrote to me.

He wrote in his letter that he had come to realize how much he had messed up his life and he understood if I never wrote back.

"God holds in His hands the workings and inter-workings of the forces of the universe, and is able to bring into play powers that we know nothing about to supplement and control those we do not know about." - Henry Halley

You can make a tremendous difference in someone's life.

We sing:
*Lord, send out your Spirit,
And renew the face of the earth.*

You can renew your life and the lives of those around you. No situation is hopeless and no one is too far gone. That young man was converted in jail and now lives a productive life with a beautiful family.

There is power in prayer!

Remember the Law

❄

Before the crossing of the Jordan, God encourages
Joshua to be Strong and Courageous, and remember
the Law, which Moses commanded them. *Joshua 1*

The Law. The Promise of God.

Don't allow God's word to be out of your
mouth or out of your mind. It will lead to happy
achievement and it will lead to prosperity.

For those of us who are grounded in
word of God will surely be:

- Firmly rooted in life. Like a tree planted by a river of life.
  - Frutifull in life. Bearing good fruit in its season.
- Will flourish in life and provide shade to those in need.

Like a tree whose leaf does not wither. They will be a place of
refreshment and encouragement for others. *Psalm 1:3 NASB*

Growing up, we used to picnic under the "Old Oak Tree"
on Salisbury Park Drive. It was this old decrepit tree in my
neighborhood. My brothers, Charlie and Andrew, my sister
Robin, and our neighbor "Brownie" and I; all used to have
picnics underneath that tree and climb its limbs. We would
play football in its shade and enjoy that tree. It would be
bare in the winter, but we always saw it. We look back on
it now, 50+ years later and we still feel fondly of that tree.

I want to be like that old oak tree. Standing tall in all seasons. A place where people gather and are refreshed and delighted. A place that people will remember fondly 50 years later and will say "Wasn't he grand to be around?"

Know Your Season

Where ever you are right now, you are in a season. You are in a season geographically, emotionally, and spiritually. Nowhere, and no one is one hundred percent status-quo the whole year round. Everything changes everywhere.

"As long as the earth lasts there will always be a time to plant and a time to gather. As long as the earth lasts there will always be cold and heat; there will always be summer, and winter, day and night." Genesis 8:22 NIV

Our lives go through seasons too. Some of those seasons are challenging. I know. Learn to appreciate every season regardless how harsh.

When my mother was sick, she asked me to drive her do some errands. Her cancer had spread to the brain and she couldn't drive. While we were driving she gave me the best advice:

"Terence, you are a good Dad. I can see you enjoy your children. (At the time I had two children, Jaimie and Josh). Don't let things like money and anxiety destroy that joy. This is the best time of your life. I loved it when you kids were young. Remember when you were young, and I would take you and your cousins to the park? I loved those days.

And when your children are older, and you can play with them as toddlers, and then help them in school; that's the best part of your life. When your children

155

are teenagers, they may drive you crazy, and you guys
drove me crazy. But that's the best time in your life.

And then, when your children are grown, and you
can relate to them parent to parent, like we are
doing now, that's the best time in your life."

My mother was telling me that no matter what season
I was in, it was the best season, because it was the
season I was in. I never forgot that advice. Never.

The next day, my mother died.
My gift to you is her advice.

On my 60th birthday, my daughter wrote me this letter. It
leads me to believe that I have lived my mother's advice.

Happy 60th Birthday to the man. Happy birthday to the
first man that Loved me, the first man that I Loved. Happy
birthday to the man that showed me how to be Loved. Happy
birthday to the man who taught me how to play guitar, to
the man who taught me how to write. Happy birthday to
the man whose radio show I used to co-host with every
Saturday morning with chocolate milk, or go to the post
office every week and get gobstoppers. Happy birthday to
the man who used to drive me an hour to school and back
and help me with my school work and resumes for college.
Happy birthday to the man whom I could charm into getting
whatever animal I like, whether it be kitten, puppy, bird,
fish, frog, hermit crab, rabbit, hamster etc. Happy birthday
to the man who inspires me. Happy birthday to the man who
took me to my first concert, to the man that took me to my
first hockey game, to the man who used to be my teammate
on mario tennis. Happy birthday to the man who always

encouraged me to continue my passion of music and art. Happy birthday to the man who has made me laugh and who has comforted me. Happy birthday to the man who gave me a great childhood, to the man who told me I was beautiful every single day and that I could be anything I wanted to be. Happy birthday to the man that has given me so much, and means more to me than I could ever express on here. Happy Birthday to my Dad. (used by permission)

This book was created over a span of twenty-five years. However, I did not start out to write a book. I was writing short devotions for my radio show. I love the rich lessons of the seasons, so I decided to arrange these devotions in seasons.

We are always in a season. Physically, or emotionally. Sometimes, it takes a keen eye to recognize the season, a wise soul to appreciate the season, and a diligent heart to perform the proper work in season.

God Bless!

I would like to thank Bob and Nancy Wick of WYRS for airing my radio all of these years.

It's still the coolest thing I have ever done.

Also, my wife Jennifer for her support and encouragement.